As a storyteller, speaker, and coach, Angela has dedicated her life to helping others discover their true selves. Yet the discovery is only the beginning. The real work begins when Angela dares her clients to step into the "space between", where they learn the power of experiencing experiences as they occur. As an internationally recognized Master Certified Coach, Advanced Certified Team Coach, and Accredited Coaching Supervisor, Angela has expertise in working with global organizations. Angela leverages her decades of corporate experience and her Master's in Education and Organizational Learning to strategically guide executives in creating leadership-culture-brand integrity.

This book is dedicated to all those who dare to choose the red pill.

Angela Cusack

DISCOVER THE MATRIX

Integrity: The True Mark of Leadership

AUSTIN MACAULEY PUBLISHERS™

LONDON • CAMBRIDGE • NEW YORK • SHARJAH

Ordering Information
Quantity sales: Special discounts are available on quantity purchases by corporations, associations, and others. For details, contact the publisher at the address below.

Publisher's Cataloguing-in-Publication data
Cusack, Angela
Discover the Matrix

ISBN 9781685624071 (Paperback)
ISBN 9781685624088 (Hardback)
ISBN 9781685624095 (Audiobook)
ISBN 9781685624101 (ePub e-book)

Library of Congress Control Number: 2022923164

www.austinmacauley.com/us

First Published 2023
Austin Macauley Publishers LLC
40 Wall Street, 33rd Floor, Suite 3302
New York, NY 10005
USA

mail-usa@austinmacauley.com
+1 (646) 5125767

A Personal Note of Gratitude

I've been writing this book in my head and heart for more than 20 years. It's a culmination of insights and wisdoms I've witnessed, learned, and now pass on to executives and organizations, entrepreneurs, and coaches I work alongside. I am writing this book now because now I am ready to step aside and grant myself permission to share the secrets that live just out of view for most, and yet, are the very one's leaders and organizations need to achieve peak performance.

This book would not have been possible without the unconditional love, support, and encouragement of my family, friends, and clients. Each one of you has played a unique role in its unfolding.

As someone who believes in dreamers' dreams, fairy tales, and miracles, I knew one day I would eventually find you, Sean Cusack. I am incredibly privileged to live this life alongside you. Being in love with you and us is what has made it possible for me to Trust My Wings and take flight. Our love gave me the courage to remove my invisibility cloak and step fully into the light. It dared me to listen to the music of my own voice and grant my fingers permission to dance freely across the keyboard as Discover the Matrix took shape. In the co-created stillness arose an undeniable spaciousness from whence I was able to capture and collect the whispers of wisdom beyond myself.

You, and our Havanese pup Murphy Rose, had to endure listening to every word as it emerged. You did so with grace, enthusiasm, and sincerity. You pushed me to not compromise my own voice and to remain fearless in my writing. It is because of you, and your unending belief in me, this book is even possible. I am forever in love with you and our ebullient love affair.

To my daughter, Courtney Robinson, with whom I share my love of storytelling, ideation, words and writing, you were the first to encourage me to write a book. From a very early age, you kindly pretended to listen to my work adventures as I drove you to and from school, and sporting events, and dropped you off at the home of friends. You offered me a safe space to think out loud, imagining book titles and themes. I can still hear you say, "Mommy, one day you will write an amazing book. And one day soon I know you'll stand on the TEDx stage sharing your insights. The world is ready for you!" I recall thinking, and secretly hoping you were right…maybe…just maybe I will.

As you grew, so did I, and on the day you were accepted and entered the coveted Virginia Commonwealth University Brand Center in 2018 to pursue your dreams, I knew that it was time for me to take the risk and pursue mine. If you dared to walk the fine line…then so would I.

Courtney, I am and will forever be grateful that you chose me to be your mom. You've taught me so much about life and more importantly about myself. I love you. You are my ever-constant and present reminder to always Dream Big, Believe Relentlessly, and Make Magic! Forever we have the stars: Starlight. Starbright.

Your gift arrived at precisely the right moment Dr. Shannon Cusack Hoskins. It was just what I needed on that Saturday morning in February 2021, as I sat staring at my computer awaiting the whispers of wisdom to return. The doorbell rang. I opened the door and accepted a tubular package from the gentle FedEx driver. After closing the door, I immediately opened the tube. With tenderness, I pulled out a small poster that contained the perfect message. This message reminded me of the importance of my work and today it hangs on the wall next to my desk. It says: "This is the season she will make beautiful things, not perfect things, but honest things that speak to who she is and who she is called to be." MHN

Thank you for believing in me always. I'm incredibly lucky and blessed that you chose to become my daughter well after you were grown. There's not a day that goes by that I don't celebrate you and the closeness of our relationship. My heart is filled with much love for you. We are forever a family of four.

Your laughter drew me in. Your witty intelligence, gentle soul, and love for all that is possible are what made us fast friends. Clare Sautter, you are a gift to me and this world. It's hard to believe that our best friend status extends well beyond 25 years. We've pulled each other up and out of some crazy dark places. We've celebrated big and small accomplishments together. We've journeyed near and far to see one another. I know I can always count on you to give me what I need when I need it. Your insights, guidance, encouragement, frank feedback, and swift kick in the pants always get me moving. You simply get me. So much of who I am is a result of our friendship and the adventures we've shared. I can't imagine life without you. You helped me discover my muse within the Matrix. Forever, I will be grateful for being with you on this journey of discovery. Thank you, my dearest friend Clare, for being you and for honoring the me that I am.

Entrepreneur and business owner extraordinaire, Mark Franko, you were the spark that single-handedly launched Igniting Success® on that cool March morning in 2011. Neither of us could have ever imagined what would transpire over a large pot of freshly ground French Press coffee. Nor did we know it would be the first of many more. We left that morning with me joining you in service on a local non-profit board, and you becoming my first client post leaving my corporate job. I cannot thank you enough for your service to our beloved community, our partnership in the evolution of your award-winning residential construction company, Mark Franko Custom Building, and most importantly our friendship. I wouldn't be where I am without you, my friend.

C.T. Hill, I can't help but smile when I think of you and our work at Crestar/SunTrust Mid-Atlantic. This book in large part is dedicated to you. Your integrity as a man, husband, father, grandfather, and leader of leaders is above all I've ever met. I had a front-row seat day-in and day-out for 8+ years and witnessed how you handled challenging rate environments, client concerns, and developed high-performing teams. The impact of your leadership and your community involvement continues to affect positive change.

In 2004, during my performance review, I asked to spend more time in Finance as I wanted to better understand where the raw data originated. I could easily interpret the data and speak about it so it could be understood by others given my many years in the business, but I felt I was missing something that would make me an even better leader. You, on the other hand, had a different idea. You listened, and after what seemed to be a long pause asked, "What it might be like if I were known as the greatest leadership coach ever?" I was stunned. I didn't see that coming. I remember a lot about that moment and the days that followed, but suffice it to say, it is you who illuminated the path I am now on. You saw my potential, encouraged me, and offered me a place on the executive team to make a difference with our teammates, clients, and community. The trust you placed in me lives in my bones.

Connie Pheiff, I refuse to even consider where I'd be without you. My guess is I'd still be generating book ideas for everyone else.

Our chance introduction in 2019 changed my life. The conversation I thought we were going to have – being a guest on the renowned Connie Pheiff Show – quickly shifted to becoming a speaker under the TCAA® label. You saw in me a possibility I had yet to sense. I had something to offer this world that was bigger than just being a guest on your show. With your guidance, I began to envision myself as a keynote speaker who would inspire and ignite human potential and bring about a positive impact on organizational cultures and brands. I would share the secrets I collected over the last 30+ years from the many CEOs and their teams, entrepreneurs, and family-owned businesses that I had been privileged to work alongside. And then the Pandemic. You had me pivot. Your encouragement to simply write my inspirations down as a way of curating my experiences was the impetus for this book and the ones that follow. Trusting in you helped me trust myself. Your weekly encouragement to simply write, and your enthusiasm for what I was bringing to life on the pages were instrumental in its emergence. Thank you for supporting me in realizing my potential as a speaker and now author. You are your brand. You lead with heart and your company is the Artist Agency With Heart®. I am incredibly grateful for our continued partnership.

There was risk in writing this book and there is risk in publishing a first-time author. Austin Macauley

Publishers™, thank you for taking the chance. Your expertise and guidance throughout the process have been exceptional.

To my faithful and forever FLGs – Elizabeth Ford and Theresa Lewis. Your unconditional love, encouragement, and boundless energy are always just the momentum I need to remember that I am always enough. Even though we are in different stages in our life, we always find a way to come together and celebrate one another wholeheartedly. I always feel supported and loved by you. Thank you for being with me on this journey.

And to my baby brother, Ray McDaniel, an extraordinary leader who wins the hearts and minds of others with ease. Ray, like myself, discovered the secrets of the Matrix long before we understood they were secret to others.

Integrity, respect, and trust are the basis of our humble existence thanks to our upbringing. Although the running joke in our family has been that I wanted to send you back to heaven when you were born, the truth is, a day doesn't go by I don't feel incredibly lucky to have you in my corner, always holding my hand through thick and thin. You are the perfect mix of our mother, Mary Sue (Roush) McDaniel and our father, Ronnie McDaniel. Their whispers are ever more present every time we speak. Ray, like you, mom and dad are embedded within the pages of this book as is our grandmother, Anna Lou (Young) Roush with whom I model myself after every day. Without the richness of your love for me and life, I wouldn't have had the confidence to step into the light.

Thank you, my readers, for choosing to step courageously into the Matrix and discover the secrets that lie within the "space between". Enjoy your journey and know I am always with you.

– Angela

Table of Contents

Introduction

The InterFlow Model™ for Leadership, Culture and Brand Alignment

A model offers a mental map for ordering complex data and experience. Within the model that follows, there are specific "mini-models" embedded which we will cover in detail. You will note that for leader, team, and organizational potential to be actualized, the ideas that are presented here must be translated into language and behaviors that can be easily communicated and incorporated in its specific working culture and context. More to come on this.

The InterFlow Model™ shown here is the foundation of *Discover the Matrix* Volume I, II, and the Field Book.

INTERFLOW MODEL™

Leadership Integrity
Defines the Quality of Leadership
(Brand)

Visible

Intangible Qualities
Invisible

Collective Intelligence
Defines the Quality of Culture
(Brand)

Visible

Organizational Culture

Customer Experience=Employee Experience

Brand Promise

Leadership Integrity

Internal Self

Space Between

External Self (Brand)

The InterFlow Model™ depicts a flowing into the other, a mixing together and a continuous reciprocal movement. This flow is always present, whether we realize it or not. It is present within our leadership, our team and organizational culture, and brand. The question is "What is the state and quality of its flow?"

Within these pages we take an intentional look vertically into our "space between" where we assess the state and quality of our integrity as leaders and as human beings. **I believe that our integrity is the single most important quality that we, as leaders, must possess for a sustainable future together.**

If we fail to align ourselves first, we simply cannot align our teams, organizations, and brand. To believe otherwise is simply foolish. Leaders are the impetus for what happens. Leaders not only generate but also initiate the InterFlow. Trust, humility, agility, resiliency are all evidenced when a leader's InterFlow is aligned. It's like magic. It's grace in motion. We follow leaders who exude the InterFlow.

On the other hand, the costs arising from our personal, organizational and brand integrity not being aligned are costly. We put ourselves in danger when our Collective Intelligences plateau. When this happens, the InterFlow of our creativity, innovation and imagination for our future is dulled and reduced to only solutioning based on what we know.

This is preventable. We simply must commit to doing the work of the InterFlow daily. For example, pausing to reflect on one's own actions in relationship to others, provides us with a unique opportunity to notice if our intentions match the impact or outcome desired. We know this by how the other person reacts. If our intentions and impact align, then we are acting in integrity. If there is a mismatch, we are out of our own alignment and likely will fall victim to our ego whose job is to defend, blame, and judge the other person for not seeing our best intentions. Don McMinn says it best, "We judge ourselves by our intentions and others by their behavior."

We must be vigilant in attending to what is critically important; the state and quality of our integrity.

Integrity – the True Mark of Leadership

You're looking for three things, generally, in a person— intelligence, energy, and integrity. And if they don't have the last one, don't even bother with the first two.
I tell them:

Everyone here has the intelligence and energy; you wouldn't be here otherwise.

But the integrity is up to you.

– Warren Buffett

Volume I of **Discover the Matrix** is dedicated to *Leadership Integrity*. Here we define and explore the implicit aspects of leadership integrity and how discovering this "space between" allows you, as an executive leader, to effectively

Align the inner world of your beliefs, ethics, commitments, values and desires with your actions and behaviors in the outer world.

In other words, leadership integrity is a state of mind and a way of being. It is not situational.

23

High integrity executive leaders have a deep commitment to do the right thing for the right reason, regardless of the circumstances. Leaders who live in integrity are incorruptible and incapable of breaking the trust of those who have confided in them. As humans, we are born with a conscience and possess the ability to know right from wrong. Choosing the right, regardless of the consequence, is a hallmark of integrity.

There's an inextricable link between integrity and trust that cannot be overestimated in the leader-employee relationship. "Executive leaders are judged on their character and competence," said David M. Long, assistant professor of Organizational Behavior at the Mason School of Business at the College of William and Mary. He further says, "Character includes integrity and signals if the leader is friend or foe. Competence signals if the leader has the ability to act on his character. A leader who has integrity and competence is a very valuable asset to [their] organization."

If you compromise your integrity in small situations with little consequence, then it becomes even easier to compromise on larger, more significant ones.

The Latin word for integrity is *Integrtatem* meaning soundness or wholeness. A leader with integrity is therefore solid and whole; not two-faced or flaky, it's more "what you see is what you get" with them. It is one of the reasons people describe leaders with integrity like a rock-solid foundation. Conversely, a leader who lacks integrity is not perceived as solid, dependable, or reliable.

All great leaders have integrity as a primary attribute. Think about those you admire most. Do they express what they believe—reflecting honesty, and what they feel—reflecting authenticity? Are they courageously open without exaggeration or misrepresentation? My bet is they do. Furthermore, they hold a deep belief in these core tenets:

- It is more important to say what I believe than to be popular.
- Things tend to always work out when I tell the truth.
- I would never lie just to get something I want from someone else.
- My life is guided and given meaning by my values.
- I always follow through on my commitments, even when it is difficult.
- I dislike those who pretend to be what they are not.
- It is always important to be open and honest about my feelings.

When an executive leader demonstrates integrity, they draw others to them, like a bee to honey, because they are trustworthy and dependable. They can be counted on, are principled and behave honorably under any situation. Because they live in integrity, they inspire others by bringing all of who they are to work, and their positive impact is felt by everyone around them. It should not be surprising then that an executive leader's integrity impacts their organizational culture, performance, profitability and brand which is the conversation we will cover in **Discover the Matrix, Volume II**.

Now, turn the page and take the first steps toward *Discovering What Lies Within the Matrix.*

Preparation for Making the Invisible Visible

Help is always around us. It is simply a matter of whether we are open enough to sense it, see it, and be curious enough to be drawn in to experiencing it. The solutions and ways forward for many of our cares and concerns seem to magically appear out of nowhere. We must not discount these miracles that emerge. Instead we can choose to appreciate that they've been there all along and it is in the moment of pause that they appear.

Trusting oneself means leaving our judgements and assumptions based on the opinions of others, our own past experiences at the threshold. It is prohibitive to carry them into the Matrix with you. As I mentioned before, discovering the Matrix isn't enough. Crossing into the Matrix is the only path to connecting wholeheartedly with the truth of who you are so you can fully experience and express it outwardly. This congruence is necessary to live in and lead with integrity.

As such, the following experiences are an invitation for you first, then your team and organization to step into the "space between" what you can see and that you haven't noticed or seen before.

In this section, I will raise fierce doubting questions for you to dance with—what kind of dance that it becomes is totally up to you. I've become known for bringing this powerful dimension into my work with clients. It changes the conversation almost immediately revealing new venues and paths to wonder about and wander through.

Let's pause here so I can be clear; fierce doubt isn't about being cynical, to the contrary, fierce doubt raises the question about the truth—your truth—that has yet been spoken. Reflective inquiry in this way presents the intangible qualities of oneself that lie currently hidden within the Matrix.

Please accept my invitation to not rush through your work. I'm not begging you; I am making a formal request because it is important. This work isn't to be taken lightly nor dismissed if your true purpose is to realize the transformational power that living in and leading with integrity has as a leader on your team, organization, culture and brand.

You have permission to linger here as long as necessary. No one is watching the clock.

Coming back to this section time and time again brings about new insights because you are a different leader with different perspectives.

And just like the soft gentle turn of a kaleidoscope, the Matrix within is always changing, creating new brilliant images of what is possible beyond our imagination.

Taking this pause to look and rest into ourselves illuminates our brilliance, a creative, unique brilliance that is just waiting to be shared with others.

I hope you will bravely discover yours and share passionately with others.

The world needs you now more than ever.

Approaching the Threshold

The Cambridge Dictionary defines threshold as "a point at which something starts; the part of a floor at the entrance to a building or room; the level or point at which you start to experience something, or at which something starts to happen or change; at the start of a new and important time or development."

As we approach the threshold, we realize that this journey isn't for the faint of heart. We begin to realize, maybe for the first time, that this path, the one we are now on, chose us.

But how?

Why?

And then in an instant, our questions illuminate a choice: Approach or turn away from the threshold that is coming into focus.

Our bodies feel the trepidation that is building with each breath we take. Stepping forward, to either side, backward or standing in stillness the choice does not disappear, it only becomes even more pronounced.

Am I ready?

What might I discover if I choose to cross and enter the Matrix?

What if I don't like what is revealed?

Can I ever go back to not knowing?

These questions are just a few of those we face.

In the background, our internal chatter fires off rapidly—one after another—like popcorn popping over an open flame. Just as the last thought pops then the next one comes again and again until we are overwhelmed with the noise. This intensity continues until it reveals the magic of the heat…what once was a hard kernel of corn is now a vulnerable, soft, open kernel that can be fully enjoyed.

It is here, in the heat of not knowing that we must become comfortable with the flame of discomfort. It is here we wonder and wander in the discovery of ourselves as leaders and all the while transforming ourselves into leaders with whom others deem is worth following.

This divine space we cultivated is one of deeper understanding about how life works. We begin to see what truly matters. In this discovery of Self, we realize it is not a tangible or physical discovery, but one that is intangible, rich with meaning, purpose, and passion: A desire for interconnectedness. The focus turns from form to function, from visible to invisible, from me to we to the world.

Chapter One
Shake Up

As a child, I had a fascination for kaleidoscopes.

I fondly remember peeking through the small opening at one end of the cardboard cylinder; peering in to witness the magic that was nestled inside.

Depending on the quality of the light that reflected off the mirror that was held in place at the far end, a variety of beautiful vivid, bright colored shapes moved together in seamless harmony, ebbing and flowing together—one after the other. I never grew tired of the mosaic of new images that appeared as I gently turned the cylinder with each image being more spectacular than the last.

I made many discoveries as I played with the kaleidoscope. The stillness, intention, ease and wonder all made my experience with this toy even more precious; a sense of intrigue, an aliveness that inspired imagination for what might be possible beyond what I knew and even what I could see.

When a particular image appeared in the cylinder with the shapes and colors coming together just perfectly, I would run into the room to share it with my grandmother. Unbeknownst to me, as I ran, the view held within this tiny cylinder was no more…in place of it was a new mosaic, one that was just as beautiful, but nonetheless very different. Mostly disappointed, I would stand in our farmhouse kitchen trying my darndest to explain the beautiful image to her.

I vividly recall how my grandmother would stop everything and carefully take the kaleidoscope in her earthy hands wrinkled from age and would look inward, standing in stillness, the silence captivating as I held my breath for her report. After viewing the image, she would look down and ask me what I had seen before beginning to share the images that were revealed to her. Our conversations were brief yet filled with inquiry. After our exchange, she would very gently hand the toy back to me and ask, "So now what do you see?" As I peered inside, I desperately wanted to see exactly what she had shared...instead, I often saw something different leaving me feeling both confused and curious.

Power of Disruption

My grandmother served as my first CEO, teaching me many valuable lessons. One of the most important was the introduction to the power of disruption; even with its unpredictable nature and its moments of perpetual frustration—it is an unbelievable gift. I learned that disruption leads us to new discoveries about ourselves, deeper connections with others and a clearer sense of who I am becoming as a leader...and more importantly as a human. The simple shaking of the canister where these tiny, mismatched pieces were contained evoked new beauty each and every time—not because I placed them there in some preconceived way, but because I allowed them to exist as they did.

Clayton Christensen, a Harvard Business School professor in the 1990s, is known as the father of "disruptive innovation," the idea that the most successful innovations are those that create new markets and value networks, thereby upending existing ones. There are volumes and volumes of research and evidence that shows "disruptive thinking" improves the odds of success—whether that be in leadership, products, services, organizations, communities or even countries. Looking at this through the lens of leadership, we can see that it is critically important to allow space for the emergent strategy to form from the disruption. Wonderment, curiosity and flexibility are required leadership attributes when engaging in disruptive thinking and innovation because often, we cannot see the end from the beginning.

A leader also has to know what their disruptive strengths are. These are the unconventional strengths that make you the best version of you. In my case, the reason I am often referred to as an organization's secret weapon is what psychologist Howard Gardner calls "searchlight intelligence: the ability to discern connections across spheres and see opportunities for cross-pollination." This is what I reference as the "space between"; the opening to discovering the Matrix.

My grandmother gave me the first glimpse of what it was to sense into the "space between." As I further reflect on my own development and that of the executive leaders I advise and coach, interview and work alongside, the challenges that we face today are many times brand new to us. We are having to let go of how we know to lead as we move into the unknown and discover the new Matrix of knowing. Although, these unprecedented times show no signs of slowing. We can rely on these truths:

- The future is coming at us faster and with far less certainty, such that the sense of "now" is even more overwhelming.
- Environment complexity is rising as fast or faster than our developmental complexity.
- Vertical development (*transformation of how we think, feel, and make sense of the world*) requires time and energy that most do not believe they have.
- A persistent false hope exists that horizontal development *(building competencies such as communication, conflict resolution, technical expertise)* will lead us out of challenging and unfamiliar circumstances in new and innovative ways.

Even now, as I prepare to publish this book, we are in the throes of inflation and on the verge of a likely recession that is different than we've experienced before. We must be careful to not lean into our recency bias and believe the same recession playbook from days before will be effective, because it will not. This, on the heels of our slow emergence from the single biggest disruption our world has ever experienced: a global health pandemic, COVID-19. During the height of the pandemic, our experiences were no longer familiar as we had to adapt hour-by-hour, day-by-day, week-by-week to the unexpected. Our evolution as individuals and communities all across the globe focused on slowing the spread of the virus. We were scared and asking questions that could only be speculated, and not easily answered. Then…on May 25, 2020, millions were awoken to another pandemic, one that has been with us for centuries. For some, racial injustice and social inequities lived in the background, for many others, it was ever present. Yet on this day, there was no looking away as media outlets played and replayed the tragic and unnecessary death of George Floyd. The unrest that followed continues to propel us forward with what I hope is a new found appreciation and understanding arising from new conversations. Conversations about our collective past and present, so we generate a new future that eliminates inequities and injustice. The timing of both pandemics may be simply good fortune. However you think about it, one thing is for sure, that as these pandemics collided, it required a new leadership to emerge.

Just as our kaleidoscope has been tossed around, a new image is coming into view. Yet, we hang on tightly to wanting to go back to the original image that we had lived in—although maybe not as beautiful as we liked, at least it was familiar. Our current experiences feel unpredictable because we cannot see or experience the experiences of others. Being invisible to the naked eye, it actively influences our mindset, our moods, and our physical well-being as we attempt to make sense of the new world that is coming into view. How we develop and learn as leaders now, matters in the moment it is happening especially as we move closer to discovering the threshold of the Matrix.

Reflection in the Mirror

As my fascination grew, so did my curiosity for how the kaleidoscope actually worked; the explanation my grandmother gave did not suffice, and my mother reminded me to simply enjoy the mystery.

As a natural explorer and experimenter, one sunny summer day, as I was playing under the grapevines on our family farm, I decided to dismantle the toy. I carefully—well, the best an 8-year-old could do—dismantled the kaleidoscope in an effort to learn its secrets.

As I pulled the cylinder apart, pieces of glass fell onto the ground revealing a variety of shapes, sizes, colors and textures. With even more curiosity, I eagerly peeked inside the cardboard tube only to find something very unexpected: a small mirror carefully anchored in place. Instead of solving the mystery, the mystery now had me firmly in its grip.

Leadership, like the kaleidoscope, has many mysteries. With more than 15,000 books and articles written on the subject and nearly 2.5 billion results when you google the word "leadership" our insatiable appetite and ongoing search for what "it" is exactly and how to do "it" is a real challenge.

In our desire to unlock the mystery, we tend to look outside of ourselves for the answers. We hunt for the ideal role model. We listen to podcasts and audiobooks any chance we get. We spend time skimming and reading articles on the subject. And we may even attend a leadership seminar on occasion if it shows promise to provide the cliff notes version on leadership. When answers do not come quickly, our interest wanes and we lead as we do while holding out hope that the secret to leadership success will magically appear.

And the secret doesn't come.

Great leaders know the outward search is very useful in gaining knowledge, expanding appreciation in their horizontal development. But they also know that is not enough.

Successful leaders know that leadership is an inside job. It requires a commitment to develop vertically and requires us to carefully dismantle our internal kaleidoscope—one piece at a time. As we do this work, we become intimately aware that the reflection of our own leadership is actually visible—it is reflected in our teams and in our organizational culture—with this insight we realize there is nowhere left to hide. The truth is undeniable. Just as the mirror within the kaleidoscope reflects a perfectly symmetrical image of what is inside, our culture reflects back the leader that we are.

I realize I am likely offering an unfavorable perspective. It is indeed a disruptive notion that breaks the image that most executive leaders affectionately have of themselves and for themselves. And yet, as I remind the many I work with and have worked with, it is simply not your fault: Leaders have been falsely led to believe that once they have the seat at the executive table they have arrived and the fault of poor results, a poor culture and poor leadership lies with those just below; it is the senior leaders who need to learn to lead, not me. And this is just simply untrue.

Exploring the *Space Between*: A Turn of the Kaleidoscope

Executive Reflection is a meta process of reflecting and then reflecting on our reflections. It requires us to ask challenging questions of ourselves, be willing to learn and continuously look for ways to improve. Executive Reflection requires a pause as we peer into our internal kaleidoscope. This "space between" involves thinking about an action, a reaction, a belief, a hypothesis or knowledge, considering it from a variety of angles and then assessing its effectiveness in moving us forward.

Indulge yourself in these questions:

1. Think back over your lifetime, when did you first experience the power of disruption?
2. What are you deliberately doing to disrupt your own career so that you don't derail?
3. Is your head up and are you aware of shifting winds inside and outside your organization?
4. Does your executive team have an aligned view of disruption?
5. Is your strategy focused on leveraging disruption?
6. Are your teams and key stakeholders committed to taking action?

If you can't see a path to your own disruption, find one, before someone else does it for you. And always be mindful of the adage, "Act, or be acted upon."

Chapter Two
Mind "Your" Gap

I'll never forget the first time I traveled abroad. After arriving at London's Heathrow airport, I grabbed my carry-on bag and headed to the subway. The thought of meeting up with my very dear friend, who was working in London at the time, and with whom I would be staying with during my impromptu visit, was exhilarating.

With instructions in hand, I proceeded toward London's underground train, affectionately known as the Tube, it was there that I saw for the first time the iconic phrase, "Mind the Gap." Being somewhat tired from the overnight flight, I recall a sense of bewilderment of what it meant outside the obvious, to watch your step; I was even more curious why, in fact, it had been placed there to begin with.

Later that evening, I met up with my friend, sharing my experience of my first intercontinental flight, arriving by Tube, and then finding my way through the quaint city streets to the hotel. In the midst of my sharing and excitement, I stopped abruptly recalling my question from earlier. Without missing a beat, I quickly asked her to tell me the story behind the message that was clearly marked wherever passengers entered and exited the train.

She burst into laughter, saying "Oh yes! I forgot to mention that to you." From our conversation, I learned the Tube is the oldest rapid transit system in the world. In 1968, well over 100 years after it was opened, a recorded voice was installed to warn those boarding and exiting the train to watch out for the "space between" the platform and train; instructing people to "mind the gap" each time a train stops system wide.

So the obvious isn't so obvious, I thought to myself.

Minding the gap has become a gentle reminder to look, pay attention and attend to what is in front of you even as it fades into the background of the daily lives of those who board and exit the Tube frequently. Yet for me, as a visitor, it was novel and in full view.

To evoke awareness and even lightness in my client engagements, upon returning back to the States, I began asking "How are you minding 'your' gap today?" This question has become a simple suggestive invitation to remind them (and me too) to become aware, fully present and responsible for managing our own "space between" as we engage with one another.

Seeing as We Are

The prominent writer, Anaïs Nin, reminds us, "We don't see things as they are, we see them as we are."

In the movie *The Truman Show,* actor Jim Carey plays a man whose entire life is a television show that is broadcast to millions but completely unknown to Truman himself. From his point of view, he is just living his life. In the middle of the movie, a group of reporters' interview "the director" played by Ed Harris who literally determines Truman's life, including whether it will rain or be sunny, the storyline for next week's show and how things will turn out for him. In this interview, one of the reporters asks the director, "How do you explain that Truman has never figured out that his whole life is just like a television show?" The director responds, "We all accept reality as it is presented to us."

Like Truman, our awareness presents itself as immediate and unmistakable. We do not stop to question the frame we put around our life, let alone whether or not it is actually the truth. We simply live our life as it presents itself. Yet in the "space between" our thoughts and actions, our assumptions, generalizations and images shape our worldview and, in turn, impact our behavior.

Our implicit biases shape our preconceptions of how things are or should be. They dramatically alter how we perceive others, situations, problems, ourselves and the world. Our thoughts and feelings quietly reside in the background of our lives and remain carefully out of sight; informing our every move regardless of whether we are unaware of them or happen to mistake them purely as a part of our personality. This is why two people may witness exactly the same event yet have vastly different perceptions.

The work in neuroscience has found that most of our actions occur without conscious thought, allowing us to function and move more freely in our extraordinarily complex world. However, science also shows that we tend to make all sorts of mental errors that are commonly referred to as cognitive biases. These biases can lead us to extrapolate information from the wrong sources, seek to confirm existing beliefs or failing to remember events the way they actually happened. Our implicit biases are so prevalent that they often predict how we will behave more accurately than our conscious values.

These mental shortcuts are neither good nor bad; they just are. They can be helpful, and conversely, they can also derail our success in relationships, innovation and performance. For example, our expedience bias moves us to make decisions swiftly which can be very useful if we are in a burning building. On the other hand, when giving 360-degree feedback to a direct report, leaning into this bias can be a huge disadvantage; compromising the working relationship.

Remember what I said earlier, our biases distort our perceptions of what is real. Therefore, identifying our biases is a very important part of the self-awareness journey that leads us to becoming more emotionally intelligent human beings, as well as better leaders.

Bring the Background into the Foreground

Being experienced as a CEO, executive, senior or front-line leader that others respect, value and are excited to follow, requires you to be intentional in identifying your known and unknown cognitive biases; bringing them to the foreground for further examination. Expanding one's self-awareness is a never-ending journey of discovery that includes not only understanding how biases impact our thoughts, behaviors, actions and decision-making, but also recognizing the ones that we tend to rely on most.

Whether it has been obvious before now or not, the reality is:

Who you are is how you lead and this is, in fact, your brand; not your self-perception of your own leadership.

The following list, taken from the *School of Thought*, contains the top 24 cognitive biases that shape our perception of reality.

As you go through the list, take your time with each one. Determine which ones most influence the way you think, behave and act before moving on to the next chapter.

Just world hypothesis. Your preference for a just world makes you presume that it exists.

A world in which people don't always get what they deserve, hard work doesn't always pay off and injustice happens is an uncomfortable one that threatens our preferred narrative. However, it is also the reality.

A more just world requires understanding rather than blame.

Remember that everyone has their own life story, we're all fallible and bad things happen to good people. Instead of pointing at something or someone externally for what feels like bad luck, turn your attention inward, replace the emotions of blame and shame with acceptance and understanding.

In-group bias. You unfairly favor those who belong to your group.

We presume that we're fair and impartial, but the truth is that we automatically favor those who are most like us, or belong to our groups.

Try to imagine yourself in the position of those in out-groups; whilst also attempting to be dispassionate when judging those who belong to your in-groups.

Fundamental attribution error. You judge others on their character, but yourself on the situation.

If you haven't had a good night's sleep, you know why you're being a bit slow; but if you observe someone else being slow you don't have such knowledge and so might presume them to just be a slow person. It's not only kind to view others' situations with charity, it's more objective too.

Be mindful to also err on the side of taking personal responsibility rather than justifying and blaming.

Halo effect. How much you like someone, or how attractive they are, influences your other judgments of them.

Our judgments are associative and automatic, and so if we want to be objective we need to consciously control for irrelevant influences. This is especially important in a professional setting.

If you notice that you're giving consistently high or low marks across the board, it's worth considering that your judgment may be suffering from the halo effect.

Anchoring. The first thing you judge influences your judgement of all that follows.

Human minds are associative in nature, so the order in which we receive information helps determine the course of our judgments and perceptions.

Be especially mindful of this bias during financial negotiations such as houses, cars and salaries. The initial price offered is proven to have a significant effect.

Sunk cost fallacy. You irrationally cling to things that have already cost you something.

When we've invested our time, money or emotion into something, it hurts us to let it go. This aversion to pain can distort our better judgement and cause us to make unwise investments.

To regain objectivity, ask yourself: Had I not already invested something, would I still do so now? What would I counsel a friend to do if they were in the same situation?

Confirmation bias. You look for ways to justify your existing beliefs.

We are primed to see and agree with ideas that fit our preconceptions, and to ignore and dismiss information that conflicts with them.

Think of your ideas and beliefs as software you're actively trying to find problems with rather than things to be defended.

"The first principle is that you must not fool yourself— and you are the easiest person to fool."

– Richard Feynam

Dunning-Kruger effect. The more you know, the less confident you're likely to be.

Because experts know just how much they don't know, they tend to underestimate their ability; but it's easy to be over-confident when you have only a simple idea of how things are.

"The whole problem with the world is that fools and fanatics are so certain of themselves, yet wiser people are so full of doubts."

– Bertrand Russell

Check yourself. Notice if you tend to overestimate your own level of skill while failing to recognize genuine skills of others because you don't see the value of unlearning and relearning what you already believe is "the way things should be done" or the reverse. If the former, derailment is sure to follow.

Backfire effect. When your core beliefs are challenged, it can cause you to believe even more strongly.

We can experience being wrong about some ideas as an attack upon our very selves, or our tribal identity. This can lead to motivated reasoning which causes us to double-down, despite disconfirming evidence.

Keep Mark Twain's quote in mind: "It ain't what you don't know that gets you into trouble. It's what you know for sure that just ain't so."

Being too resolute about your opinions, beliefs and values can sideline you; creating an identity you may not wish you had.

Barnum effect. You see personal specifics in vague statements by filling in the gaps.

Because our minds are given to making connections, it's easy for us to take nebulous statements and find ways to interpret them so that they seem specific and personal.

Psychics, astrologers and others use this bias to make it seem like they're telling you something relevant.

Consider how things might be interpreted to apply to anyone, not just you.

Declinism. You remember the past as better than it was, and expect the future to be worse than it will likely be.

Despite living in the most peaceful and prosperous time in history, many people believe things are getting worse. The 24-hour news cycle, with its reporting of overtly negative and violent events, may account for some of this effect.

Instead of relying only on nostalgic impressions of how great things "used to be," reflect on the context of the time by gathering measurable metrics such as life expectancy, levels of crime and violence, and prosperity statistics to balance your perspective.

Framing effect. You allow yourself to be unduly influenced by context and delivery.

We all like to think that we think independently, but the truth is that all of us are, in fact, influenced by delivery, framing and subtle cues. This is why the ad industry is a thing, despite almost everyone believing they're not affected by advertising messages.

Only when we have the intellectual humility to accept the fact that we can be manipulated, can we hope to limit how much we are.

Be mindful of how things are being put to you before buying into popular narratives that frequently play into our hopes of a quick fix.

Placebo effect. If you get sick after eating a specific food, like ice cream, you may begin to associate that food with having been sick and avoid it in the future or if you take a specific pill to relieve a headache, you begin to associate it with pain relief even if the pill you just took was a sugar pill.

The Placebo effect is rooted in our expectations. If you have prior expectations of something they have the power to influence current and future perceptions of it.

Stop here. What expectations do you have about things, situations or people where the Placebo effect may be at work?

Bystander effect. You presume someone else is going to do something in an emergency situation. Take the case of George Floyd, the recent school shootings, coming the aid of someone in distress or speaking out for others who cannot speak for themselves.

When something terrible is happening in a public setting we can experience a kind of shock and mental paralysis that distracts us from a sense of personal responsibility. We stand by and watch instead of act. The problem is that everyone can experience this sense of deindividuation in a crowd and too often does. Our excuse is "someone else with more—power, knowledge, skills, etc.—will take care of it."

Make a choice now. If there's an emergency, presume to be the one who will help or call for help. Don't wait for someone else to speak up or act.

Don't simply profess to believe in the words of Mahatma Gandhi, live and practice them daily. Make a commitment to stand up for others and "Be the change you want to see in the world."

Availability heuristic. Your judgements are influenced by what most easily comes to mind. It is why when we make decisions, we tend to be swayed by what we remember. And what we remember is influenced by many things including how recent, emotionally powerful, or unusual your memories are making them seem more relevant. This, in turn, can cause you to apply them too easily. There are 3 reasons this likely happens: 1) We often misjudge the frequency and magnitude of recent experiences and events; 2) Our memories are limited about the specifics of the events; and 3) We recall things better when they come in the form of a vivid narrative and somatically visceral, where the felt sense remains alive.

By seeking different perspectives and relevant evidenced based information rather than relying purely on first judgments and emotive influences can help limiting its impact.

Curse of knowledge. Once you understand something you presume it to be obvious to everyone.

Things make sense once they make sense, so it can be hard to remember why they didn't. We build complex networks of understanding and forget how intricate the path to our available knowledge really is.

When teaching someone something new, go slow and explain like they're ten years old (without being patronizing). Repeat key points and facilitate active practice to help embed knowledge.

Now do the same when talking to your executive colleague who may not have your context, experience, and perspective on issues. Just because you both are senior leaders doesn't mean they know, have experienced, or share the same context as you. Be patient and slow down.

Belief bias. If a conclusion supports your existing beliefs, you'll rationalize anything that supports it.

It's difficult for us to set aside our existing beliefs to consider the true merits of an argument. In practice this means that our ideas become impervious to criticism, and are perpetually reinforced.

A useful thing to ask is "When and how did I get this belief? Might this belief be outdated? What information is being presented that might update my belief for the betterment of self, team and our organization?" We tend to automatically defend our ideas without ever really questioning them. When you notice yourself defending, stop and reflect on what it is you fear most.

Self-serving bias. You believe your failures are due to external factors, yet you are personally responsible for your successes.

No one wants to admit being incompetent but when we fail to recognize our lack of knowledge, skills and experiences, we find ourselves judging and blaming our current circumstances.

While many of us enjoy unearned privileges, luck and advantages that others do not. We must remain consciously diligent in listening to our internal voice that says, "I deserve things, recognition and promotion, and I'd have it if it weren't for the situation I'm in."

A critical note: Be mindful of how this bias interacts with the just-world hypothesis, fundamental attribution error and the in-group bias.

Groupthink. You let the social dynamics of a group situation override the best outcomes because it feels better more to go along to get along. Our desire to "fit in" limits the quality of our voice within the group. It is true that dissent is often uncomfortable and possibly dangerous to one's social standing, however, it is often the most confident or first voice that determines group decisions.

When you sense that it is easier to go along, maybe because you don't have a strong opinion, pause and wonder about the perspectives of others. Encourage a dialogue where differing points of view can be heard. Seek to facilitate objective means of evaluation, critical thinking practices and risk mitigation as a group activity before settling in and moving on.

Negativity bias. You allow negative things to disproportionately influence your thinking.

The pain of loss and hurt are felt more keenly and persistently than the fleeting gratification of pleasant things. We may experience the pleasant things as luck or good fortunate versus seeking them as they are; life experiences. It is true, we are primed for survival, and our aversion to pain can distort our judgment in a modern world.

Using pro and con lists, as well as thinking in terms of probabilities, can help you evaluate things more objectively than relying solely on initial impressions. Practice the game of speculation with others and see what possible futures you can create beyond the ones associated with your innate fear.

Optimism bias. You overestimate the likelihood of positive outcomes. A naivety gives way to healthy skepticism.

There can be benefits to a positive attitude, but it's unwise to allow such an attitude to adversely affect our ability to make rational judgments, which not mutually exclusive. Blending these polarities together allows for deeper and broader perspectives to emerge leading to better, more realistic decisions.

When we hear ourselves say, "I trust things will improve with time" and take no action to make it so, be consciously aware that you may be naively trusting yourself, the situation or another person resulting in later disappointments and frustrations. Instead of relying on hope, pause and cross-check your pattern and tendency with others and ask for their point of view.

Pessimism bias. You overestimate the likelihood of negative outcomes and lack hope or confidence in the future. You may notice a predisposition for "worse-case scenarios" in your own life as well as the lives of others.

Pessimism is a coping technique for those who have chosen to set low expectations for situations regardless of prior success. It is a defense mechanism against future disappointments which are to be prepared for and avoided at all costs.

Depression and anxiety can result from pessimism if it persists over time. Pay close attention to your thoughts while noticing how you are feeling about the world around you.

Take care of these initial thoughts by exploring them with someone you trust such as a therapist, doctor, or coach. If feelings and negative thoughts persist related to permanence, pervasiveness and being personal seek support immediately.

Reactance. This is a natural defense against presence. It occurs when someone is trying to compel you to do something, yet you experience threat and loss of control and do the opposite of what that person is trying to make you do.

When we feel our liberty is being constrained, our inclination is to resist, however, in doing so we can overcompensate leading to potential choices and decisions that may not benefit us.

When you feel that your choices are restricted, be careful not to lose your objectivity. Pause, reflect on your experience and let your internal wisdom spring forward; guiding you to make a well-informed decision.

Spotlight effect. You overestimate how much people notice how you look and act.

Most people are much more concerned about themselves than they are about you. Absent overt prejudices, people generally want to like and get along with you as it gives them validation too.

Instead of worrying about how you're being judged, consider how you make others feel. They'll remember this much more, and you'll make the world a better place.

Exploring the Space Between: Mirror. Mirror

When we stop taking for granted that "the way we see things is the way they really are," we begin "minding our gap." We open ourselves to changing our personal fixed worldview in favor of new possibilities, innovations, relationships, and expanded opportunities for how we lead our organizations, not only through the recent pandemic and social unrest but through any unimaginable challenges we might face in the future.

Executive Reflection requires us to ask challenging questions of ourselves, be willing to learn, and continuously look for ways to improve. Executive Reflection requires a pause as we reflect on our internal constructs. Turning the mirror toward ourselves allows us to discover the "space between." This discovery further entices to not just peer inside, but to step wholeheartedly into the Matrix where we may find our most authentic expression of Self. As we pause, we invite inquiry with the fullness of intellectual and whole-body curiosity that questions what and how we know what we know. This, in turn, invites us into contemplation and wonderment about what it is we do not know.

"The real voyage of discovery consists not in seeking new landscapes, but in having new eyes."

– Marchel Proust

As you move into the next chapter, bring with you an inquisitiveness to wonder:

- Why do I trust my senses to perceive the real world?
- What are biases are influencing my perceptions the most?
- What actions might I consider taking to align my own perception of my leadership with those that others have of me? Do I even know how I am perceived?

The way we see ourselves may or may not be how others experience us. We may have the right intentions to do the right things by and for others' yet somehow, we get in our own way.

Chapter Three
Skeletons in the Closet

Buried deep in the recesses of our mind, we hold secret narratives about who we are, who others are and how the world should work. We rarely, if ever, peek inside the closet for fear of what we may discover, or worse what others might discover about us. It is this perpetual fear of exposing our skeletons to the light of day that keeps us stuck, playing the same game in the same way.

The lyrics from Stevie Wonder song *Skeletons* hits the mark:

Skeletons in your closet Itchin' to come outside Messin' with your conscience in a way your face can't hide

Oh things are gettin' real funky Down at the old corral and it's not the skunks that are stinkin' It's the stinkin' lies you tell

What did your mama tell you about lies She said it wasn't polite to tell a white one What did your daddy tell you about lies He said one white lie turns into a black one

So, it's gettin' ready to blow It's gettin' ready to show Somebody shot off at the mouth and We're getting ready to know

It's gettin' ready to drop It's gettin' ready to shock Somebody done turned up the heater An' a it's gettin' ready to pop.

Crevices in your pantry Now what do we have in here Havin' a daytime nightmare Has always been your biggest fear.

Oh things are gettin' real crucial Up the old wazoo Yet you cry, why am I the victim? When the culprit's y-o-u.

Let's face it, leaving our skeletons in the shadows of a dark closet is far safer. We feel comfort in the familiarity of these stories: "This is how I am. I've done it this way for so long there is no reason to change now. They are the ones that need to get a clue, not me. If they find out the truth, they won't like me." And the more we make excuses for our skeletons, the more power we give them in defining the quality of our leadership and our life.

I've heard from plenty of executives that finding the closet where their skeletons are buried is the most difficult part. Since they didn't know they had a secret closet that held their skeletons to begin with, they rarely knew where to begin the search. Well, I say, let's begin by looking where you are not…in the "space between" what you know, how you know and why you know what you know.

In the fantasy tale written by C.S. Lewis in the 1950s' *The Chronicles of Narnia,* four children go to live with an old professor during the war and discover a wardrobe while playing hide and seek. If you recall the story, the wardrobe was in plain view. It was a typical non-descript piece of furniture that was simply overlooked.

Your wardrobe is right in front of you—and like in the story, it reveals a place filled with mysteries and magic that will afford you opportunities to push beyond yourself and achieve peak performance.

Peeking to Peak

It takes bravery to walk up to the closet door. It takes even more courage to look inside. And, like most, we may not be ready to fling back the door to face the skeletons that are inside. Yet, if we truly want to achieve our highest potential as a leader we have to begin, and beginning means bending down, focusing in, as you peek through the keyhole to reflect honestly on these questions:

- Do I have skeletons in my closet?
- When I think of them, how do I feel?
- What would I do if it, or they, became public?
- Am I adding skeletons to my closet?
- Who knows about my skeletons?
- Do they need to remain secret?

This peek is the first reveal to what is inside. Over the three decades I've worked with executives, I've discovered there tends to be one or more of the following skeletons that keep them from achieving their peak performance.

Imposter?!

Studies have estimated that nearly 70% of individuals will experience signs and symptoms of the imposter phenomenon at some point in their life. Personally, I think that number is a lot higher.

First described by Suzanne Imes, PhD and Pauline Rose Clance, PhD in the 1970s, imposter syndrome occurs among high achievers who are unable to internalize and accept their own success as theirs. In other words, it's the inability to believe you deserve or have achieved your success using your own strengths, efforts or skills. For me, the narrative behind feeling like a fraud stems from being taught that I need to work twice as hard to be half as good and while this instills a goal-oriented approach within me, it also keeps me feeling as though my efforts will never be good enough.

In our society, there are huge pressures to achieve. When we as leaders—and parents—send mixed messages alternating between over-praise and criticism about achievements, we run the risk of increasing future fraudulent feelings in others and ourselves. It is a vicious cycle. This further leads to a lot of confusion between approval and love and worthiness. When we get these confused, we begin to believe our self-worth is only contingent on achieving. As our inner critic gains strength, so do our feelings of anxiety and depression. We push the skeleton further back into the closet, our shame intensifying, preventing us from speaking about it in the light of day.

Although imposter syndrome may be with us all the time, it flares when we are in the "space between" phases of our professional development that arise from taking on new endeavors. When we experience self-doubt as we face new challenges, we discover these challenges are accompanied by a fear of being found out that we don't have what it takes. Even if we experience outward signs of success, we have trouble believing it was nothing more than pure luck. This is why we find that imposter syndrome and perfectionism often go hand in hand.

To safeguard ourselves from feeling like an imposter, we begin to think every task we tackle must be done perfectly and done alone; there is no asking for help. Asking for help is revealing the very skeleton we are trying to hide. This leads to procrastination out of fear that we won't be able to complete the assignment to the necessary standards, or we will over prepare, spending much more time on the task than is necessary. Afraid of being discovered, we will go through contortions to do a project perfectly. When we succeed, we believe all that anxiety and effort paid off; feeding into our superstition that if we don't repeat the self-imposed torture, we won't be successful.

But what if we flipped all this on its head?

The truth is imposter syndrome is normal and it can drive peak performance if you are willing to illuminate it— bring it out into the light of day. Studies show that people who worry about not being up for the job are often the very people you want to be doing the job. They care enough to do the homework and will typically only raise their hand when they feel they are 120% capable of doing the job well.

Instead of obsessing about being a fraud, use the imposter syndrome as a signal that you are on the path to learning, growing and becoming an even more capable version of yourself.

Think of your doubt as illuminating the path to your next major breakthrough.

Imperfections?!

Imperfections are those things we want to lose. They are the scars we want to hide. They are the events in our lives where we claim to be at-fault or we have failed to achieve. The stories we tell ourselves about these imperfections cloud our minds and close our hearts. We are so busy making up excuses that we do not see how these blemishes add to, not subtract from, our unique leadership tapestry.

If this is the case, then why do we try to hide our imperfections?

Simple answer: We fear rejection. Rejection of not fitting in, not belonging and worse being abandoned. Shining a light on what we are not is just too risky. For many, this skeleton has been with us hidden away since childhood.

The fear of rejection stops us from being authentic, it puts the kibosh on vulnerability. It moves us to only do things and take things on that we know we can do well. It drives us to become perfectionists where our standards are never met which translates to "not only you are not good enough but neither am I." To prevent others from finding out, we hide our imperfections in the deepest part of our closet.

The fear of being discovered means we have to constantly be on alert to bar the door, in hopes no one finds the key. All this energy has a tremendous negative impact on our ability to lead effectively. The fear of being found out puts us on the ready—code for defensiveness—all the time. And I do mean all the time. We see our leadership style as direct, candid and more often than not "right" which reinforces the need to constantly demonstrate why we are, indeed, right—why our concepts, processes, ideas are better than anyone else's ideas all to ensure our skeletons remain hidden.

On the flip side, our defensiveness is experienced by others as being a *bull in a china shop*: a person who breaks things or who often makes mistakes or causes damage in situations that require careful thinking or behavior. Teams with this kind of leader tend to stay heads down and low to the ground to avoid being shamed…and the cycle continues.

I've experienced this firsthand in the early days of my corporate career. I've seen it as an executive coach and business advisor within organizations I've worked with. These executives proudly label themselves as "tough," "a$$holes," "exterminators," "taking no bullshit" "not afraid to break things," and so on. The people around them suffer. In my corporate experience, I recall thinking that the people who reported to this highly intelligent senior executive resembled the walking dead.

Although at that point in my life, I had no ability to impact the senior executive himself, I did offer to help senior leaders who reported to him, giving them strategies to try to navigate situations when engaging in conversations with him. The most effective tip I offered was to not point out publicly how his thinking, approach or concept might be flawed. Instead, listen and nod. Come back and leave a voicemail explaining another possible option before going home or early the next day. My hunch was that he would take the idea as his own and the senior leader would end up in the right place. To my amazement it worked 100% of the time. The reality is…this was only a survival strategy not a thriving strategy. I was too young to see the difference at the time. As my experience grew, so did my wisdom for how to support senior leaders in navigating such executives and CEOs who they might encounter during their career.

Fast forward 20 years.

I'm recruited by the CEO and President of a fast growing $10B organization to work with everyone on the executive team including the CEO. The organization had a good brand reputation within the market and was considered very successful. The primary purpose for the engagement was two-fold: First, to elevate the leadership of every executive in preparation for eminent growth, and second, and most importantly, was to make this "so called" team into a team.

During my initial one-on-ones with each executive, I found nothing surprising; a variety of passions and perspectives on what was the most important for the organization to focus on. What I did find surprising was the level of excitement about working with an executive coach who had deep knowledge of the business. And then there was "the" one. I stood face-to-face with a similar persona to the one I had helped others work around 20-years earlier.

Our pleasantries quickly shifted into an abrasive hardcore "let's test this coach" conversation. Game on.

About 10 minutes in, I abruptly stopped him and asked, "So is this it? The way you lead?" Silence. Then, a response, "I know I am an a$$hole. I take pride in being this way. Everyone knows this is just how I am."

"Really, I said…well, I'll tell you this, you won't last here or anywhere else long term," as I stood up to leave.

As I approached the door of his office he said, "Stop. Come back." I turned and sat back down. In that moment I knew I was likely the only person who had ever pointed out the skeleton that was pretending to keep him safe when in reality, it only made him small.

Other leaders who shove their imperfections in the closet have refined the art of weaving together a string of "almost" truths that in any given moment become their truth. The story is forever changing, their reason and rationale sounding plausible and so we look the other way. This executive is the most difficult to confront because they just won't or can't see that any other perspective or possibility is plausible. They have high expectations of others; proclaimed perfectionists allowing them to convince themselves and others that they need to be in the weeds of every detail; their personal brand on the line.

Having coached an executive like this, at first, I was mesmerized. Her charming disposition, passion for perfection, inspiring work, knowledge of the industry and dedication to encouraging the growth in others is exactly the kind of executive that anyone would want to work for and with. The outside was not at all what was happening on the inside. As we worked together, the lies she told herself but couldn't see as lies surfaced. When confronted, it turned into a slippery slope of blame, shame and victimization. The skeletons, in this case, buried so deep in the recesses of the closet were covered with blankets and blankets of lies from which she lived her life were simply too many for me—an executive coach—to coach her through. I recommended she meet with a therapist.

The company, on the verge of having 80% of their workforce leave, made the decision to end her contract immediately. During the final meeting where I facilitated the closing conversation, she continued to deny the evidence and accepted no responsibility for the impact of her behaviors. She begged the CEO not to release her. One year after the event, the company was thriving. It took time to recover and rebuild the trust that had been seriously damaged, but the other executive leaders stood up, owning that they too were part of the problem as they looked the other way one too many times. I often remind leaders that having good intentions simply isn't good enough. Hiding behind this phrase is just another skeleton that has fallen into the "space between." Great leaders examine how their impact of their behaviors align with their intentions. And this, I claim, is the way toward living out of one's highest level of integrity.

Our imperfections are what make us human.

As Ziad K. Abdelnour, author of Economic Warfare: Secrets of Wealth Creation in the Age of Welfare Politics writes, "There's no need to be perfect to inspire others. Let people get inspired by how you deal with your imperfections." And that is what employees want from their leaders; leaders who are human, imperfections and all. And every time we, as leaders, reveal one of our imperfections, our employees feel safe to reveal one of theirs.

Leadership isn't about being perfect and we shouldn't expect perfection from our teams. Owning up to mistakes and embracing our flaws is an important part of leadership. Brennan Manning drives this point home by saying, "Be who you is, or you is who you ain't." And that's the real point. Every time leaders cover up their imperfections—pushing them to the cobweb corners of their closet—they compromise. They compromise the very thing they are seeking, their authentic Self.

Emotions?!

Emotions are a funny thing. Even saying the word, "emotions" conjures up a wide range of thoughts and biases for how we should and should not express, or even deal with the feelings that arise within us. They have been, and in some incidents still are, a neglected part of who we are. Leaders are highly skilled and often rewarded in the workplace for simply ignoring them, pushing them aside and avoiding them at all costs. Largely, being devoid of emotion has led leaders to rise to higher levels of leadership quickly, amassing more and more power that continues the culture that is both comfortable and mechanistic. Their claim of being emotionless is the only way to remain objective.

These skeletons that are confined to the closet, do sneak out from time to time. They appear under the cloak of darkness even in the light of day as tempers flare and opinions differ. The leader blaming and shaming those around them as they pick up the bones that are scattered about, shoving them swiftly, deeper and deeper into the closet in hopes that no one sees them. Out of sight, out of mind. There's no need to deal with something you don't understand.

That was me.

I grew up not needing to understand emotions. For the most part, the only emotions that were acceptable were the "good" ones, everything else required a face covering.

Feelings of sadness, anger, disappointment, frustration, shyness, laziness, anxiousness, boredom were just plain unacceptable. "People had it worse than we do" was often the phrase I heard. Or if you did something wrong or failed there was no room for excuses regardless of the depths of the suffering. Still ringing clearly in my ear, "You made your bed, now lie in it" simply means no one has time to deal with your feelings, so buck up and move on. This required living life with a permanent mask. And behind the mask a stoic face formed, expressionless until the right time in the right situation. This is how I entered the workforce.

Like many executives I work with today, I too failed at having deep connections. Ambitious, enthusiastic, persuasive with a passion for people, I became an empowering storyteller that spoke from an armored heart that successfully moved strategic imperatives, business goals and performance year over year ahead. I mastered the art of leaving my skeletons in the closet to the point I had forgotten they were even there. Thus, I rose to executive ranks.

While in the midst of keeping these secrets from myself and others, I was given reinforcing feedback that keeping my skeletons locked up was indeed a good idea if I wanted to continue my upward career progression. Fitting in meant not letting others in. What I learned later in life, thanks to a friend who cared deeply for my well-being, fearlessly told me I'd have more impact when I became a life-long commitment to developing myself beyond my perceived edges. As she spoke, my stomach turned, my heart dropped and my closet door flew open. It was at that moment I promised myself to learn and lead differently.

Our emotions are highly influenced and shaped by our heritage, family histories, social norms, cultures and our own experiences. They are the filter by which we see what and how we see and thus make meaning of the events that occur around us. They give rise to the context and quality of our narratives. Emotions live just out of sight in the "space between." And here they remain if we are unwilling and unable to recognize them, perpetuating our unconscious bias, limiting our ability to learn and without learning we cannot achieve peak performance.

In Dan Newberry and Curtis Watkins's book, *The Field Guide to Emotions: A Practical Orientation to 150 Essential Emotions* offer this interpretation:

"An emotion is what the etymology of the word suggests: e-motion. It is 'the energy that puts you in motion' or 'that which moves you.' We all can notice the energy that urges us to move faster, change position, or say something we consider important. That energy is the emotion. In this case, 'action' and 'motion' are distinct from 'movement.' An emotion such as laziness will make lying immobile on the sofa attractive, which is its particular 'predisposition to action'. Emotional energy could show up as a reaction to an experience, which would be an emotion, or it could be more long-lasting, in which case we might call it a mood."

This reframing invites us to see emotions for what they are, energy in motion. The impetus for moving or not moving action forward. From this perspective, emotions serve as a core part of our intellectual process for choosing and decisioning, and yet we continue to avoid opening the closet door.

Thanks to many management thought-leaders, emotions are now a part of our nomenclature. Emotional Intelligence, as a psychological theory, was developed by Peter Salovey and John Mayer in 1990. They said, "Emotional intelligence is the ability to perceive emotions, to access and generate emotions so as to assist thought, to understand emotions and emotional knowledge, and to reflectively regulate emotions so as to promote emotional and intellectual growth."

Five-years later, Daniel Goleman popularized the topic when he published his first book *Emotional Intelligence* where he introduced a whole new perspective on predicting and analyzing employee performance. In his seminal book, Goleman defines it as "the ability to identify, assess and control one's own emotions, the emotion of others and that of groups."

The first component of Goldman's Five Components of Emotional Intelligence is self-awareness: one's ability to recognize and understand their own personal moods and emotions as well as their impact on others. And this is where leaders must begin.

Blind Spots?!

Average leadership in good times can be covered up, but in challenging times, the skeletons come out. You've seen it happen and so have I. A talented executive hired as part of succession planning efforts to build and grow a segment of the business. In person, and on paper, this senior leader is a superstar. Their ability to come in quickly and make the changes necessary to level up the talent, change the organizational structure and improve processes to achieve organizational excellence is bar none. And then the inevitable happens. Challenges arise and the superstar goes rogue becoming ineffective unbeknownst to themselves.

Our inability to see what is right in front of us results from knowing what we know the way we know it without any consideration for other possibilities. It is born from our history of how things have been done as well as a narrow focus on where the organization is going. Executives and major companies have failed due to their blind spots.

We all have blind spots. They are the inevitable skeletons in our closet that require assistance from others to illuminate. They can be some of the most difficult to face, yet they are the ones that ultimately determine our fate.

As pointed out in a June 2009 *Harvard Business Review* article, "Ten Fatal Flaws That Derail Leaders," Jack Zenger, CEO and Joseph Folkman, President of Zenger/Folkman have shown in their research that ineffective leaders are often unaware that they exhibit these behaviors. In fact, these ineffective leaders rate themselves substantially more positively than the ratings given by their peers.

Lack energy and enthusiasm. They see new initiatives as a burden, rarely volunteer, and fear being overwhelmed. One such leader was described as having the ability to "suck all the energy out of any room."

Accept their own mediocre performance. They overstate the difficulty of reaching targets so that they look good when they achieve them. They live by the mantra, "Underpromise and overdeliver."

Lack clear vision and direction. They believe their only job is to execute. Like a hiker who sticks to the trail, they're fine until they come to a fork in the road.

Have poor judgment. They make decisions that colleagues and subordinates consider to be not in the organization's best interests.

Don't collaborate. They avoid peers, act independently, and view other leaders as competitors. As a result, they are set adrift by the very people whose insights and support they need.

Don't walk the talk. They set standards of behavior or expectations of performance and then violate them. They're perceived as lacking integrity.

Resist new ideas. They reject suggestions from subordinates and peers. Good ideas aren't implemented, and the organization gets stuck.

Don't learn from mistakes. They make no more mistakes than their peers, but they fail to use setbacks as opportunities for improvement, hiding their errors and brooding about them instead.

Lack interpersonal skills. They make sins of both commission (they're abrasive and bullying) and omission (they're aloof, unavailable and reluctant to praise).

Fail to develop others. They focus on themselves to the exclusion of developing subordinates, causing individuals and teams to disengage.

Do you recognize any of these blind spots in others? In yourself? If these skeletons are not uncovered quickly, the outcome will be a huge loss for the leader, their teams, and the organization.

Exploring the *Space Between*: Skeleton Keys

Now it's time to unlock the closet door where your skeletons lie. The keys are laying right in front of you. Will you choose to pick them up and open the door?

By not exposing our skeletons to the light of day, we remain unconsciously incompetent in how we can shift our leadership approach and style. We remain out of control and live in hopes that what we do and how we do it will continue to work. And that is never sufficient in achieving ultimate success.

Remember,

You're not stuck, you're just committed to a certain pattern of behavior because they helped you in the past. Now those behaviors have become more harmful than helpful. The reason why you can't move forward is because you keep applying an old formula to a new level in your life. Change the formula to get different results.

– Emily Maroutian

Shining a light on our skeletons allows us to overcome some deeply held beliefs we have of ourselves, namely the belief we just don't measure up because we aren't good enough.

Now it is time to practice Executive Reflection. This is where you will ask yourself the following challenging questions, and remain open to learning as you continuously look for ways to improve.

As you reflect on what follows, ask yourself?

- Will I…?
- How will I…?
- When will I…?
- What support do I need and from whom?

Give consideration to the following as you unlock the closet where the skeletons are hiding out:

Confront self-doubts. Just because you're a person who holds an executive position doesn't mean you never doubt yourself. The first step for a leader in confronting self-doubt is to acknowledge that you are experiencing it. By ignoring your self-doubts, you give them control over you and they become skeletons in your closet. When addressing self-doubts, be prepared for the doubt to become your superpower. Sometimes, just focusing on what makes you, you, begins to erode your self-doubt immediately.

Confide in the team. Setting a good example for your employees doesn't mean you have to be perfect. In fact, concealing your imperfections will only give your team unrealistic expectations. Sharing your struggles is a great way to encourage mistakes and healthy risk taking. When you are humble and express vulnerabilities, it actually comes across as courage and daring. When you share your experiences, it builds rapport, confidence and strengthens the bond for everyone. Furthermore, confiding in others shows that you trust them and value their feedback and support which creates bonds that are long-lasting.

Admit your faults. If you mess up, don't cover it up. This only sends a message to your team that it isn't ok to make a mistake which creates a very stressful environment and unnecessary tension on the team. When leaders admit their own mistakes, it communicates authenticity and humility creating a psychological safe environment where accountability for self and others organically emerge forming a strong cultural underpinning for the organization.

Accept help. You likely are offering help to others without thinking you also need help as well. The best leaders know they need help, and they are not afraid to ask for it. They accept support with gratitude and wholeheartedness. Leaders who accept help, give the other person a gift of contributing and being part of the solution as a teammate and partner, not just a follower.

Be inquisitive and reflective. Questions change answers. Answers don't change if we don't call the question. Spending time daily in Executive Reflection is paramount for Senior Executives, Presidents and CEOs. But why wait until then…begin now wherever you are in your leadership journey.

Your self-awareness journey toward developing leadership integrity has just begun.

Chapter Four
Permission to Unzip

Accept this as your permission slip.

Permission to unzip, revealing what is true for you about you. This is your permission slip to step into the arena of your life.

I can confirm that leaving the comfort of the stands can feel risky, very risky. Just the thought of unzipping, exposing our cares, expectations, beliefs, values and biases that inform our actions and decisions can be paralyzing. We find ourselves frozen while feeling safe and secure as we sit in the comfort of our own chair surrounded by others sitting in their own chairs staring into the middle waiting, watching and secretly hoping that this conversation will somehow magically be different from the others; where veiled elephants are unveiled, and real alignment is attained.

Remaining seated in the stands is a form of privately opting out from leading with and living in integrity. We fool ourselves into believing that going with the flow is not only what is expected but what is required to lead a successful life. Yet, contrary to this popular belief it is exactly what makes us look foolish and prevents us from experiencing a fulfilled, prosperous life.

On the surface, privately opting out—withholding our truth by silencing ourselves—does seem easier than publicly opting in at the moment. But under further examination, leaders who choose to accept this permission slip to unzip lead personal and professional lives in integrity and discover that in actuality, privately opting out is far more difficult.

Privately opting out requires us to not only zip back up but it also demands that we mask up, pushing our true selves further into the background where we become smaller and experience ourselves as insignificant. However, to the contrary, once we unzip and practice repeatedly unzipping a bit more each time, a level of comfort out of the initial awkwardness creates a brave space to reveal our true selves. This leaves us with a new awareness that rezipping and returning to the old narrative is not only what we do not want to do, it is almost always impossible to do.

Don't get me wrong, we can choose to write our own permission slip to privately opt out at any given moment, in any given situation because we feel at jeopardy or unsafe in some way.

However, here's my warning: If reoccurrence of the initial privately opting out becomes the predominant choice, it will, in short order, develop into a deep lingering resignation and resentment that clouds our ability to lead effectively. This deep lingering will follow us wherever we go just like the dark cloud of dust that follows Pig Pen in the classic Charlie Brown cartoon strips.

A Brave Heart

It takes a brave heart and incredible courage to shatter the illusions that we have of ourselves and fearlessly share the vulnerabilities that are just out of view. And that is what it means to step fully into our lives and lead others with integrity. We don't make it the responsibility of others to assume they know where we are coming from, we reveal it to them—openly, candidly, confidently and humbly. Our ego takes a backseat to our desire to be real with ourselves and others, even if shame momentarily arises, stings and lingers as an outcome of being blind to the impact of our behaviors that results in unnecessary suffering that we have created.

On a beautiful sunny day in March, we sat together on one of my final days of work in Miami, Florida. The incredible view across Biscayne Bay as we looked toward the Keys was simply breathtaking. A dear friend and work associate and I sat quietly for some time, as had become our ritual over the past three years, before sharing our thoughts, feelings, joys, frustrations and disappointments. We found that peace arose from simply resting together in the middle of our very busy days was a wonderful respite.

The silence was broken when my friend shifted her position on the bench toward me. She paused, took a cleansing breath and as she removed her sunglasses said, "We are all going to miss you, you know." I recall a warmth coming over me as a smile formed on my face. It was heartwarming to hear I would be missed, and in my mind, I immediately translated this to mean I had made important contributions as a member of the team; something very important to me.

The silence broken, we talked and laughed for a bit longer, desperately wanting the sadness to evaporate like the rain so often did after a sun shower. Tears began to well up in our eyes. Although I wasn't self-aware enough to notice that the sensations I was experiencing were different from others I had experienced before, I did sense that what was on the verge of happening would be profound. I just didn't realize how profound.

Facing me with her head resting on her hand supported by the back of the bench, she shared an insight that I already knew about myself: "You are one of the best listeners I've ever met. It's a gift." And then without warning, she illuminated a "space between" what I knew and what was the cause of her sadness. Her next statement shattered me. I felt such deep shame that I couldn't speak for what seemed like years. She said without hesitation, "Yet, I don't know you. I don't really know anything about you." I didn't know what to say, so I said nothing. I bowed my head retreating inward to find protection. My armored heart had been cracked open, but at the time I still didn't want to face this truth.

This story lives in my bones. In a flash, everything I had believed about myself went up in a fiery ball of flames more luminous than the sun. I had to come to terms with the real truth: I wasn't living in integrity if I was consciously or even unconsciously choosing to withhold for the sake of protecting myself in some way. I was completely zipped up. This truth further complicated my claim of being a high-integrity leader. Exactly how could I lead with integrity if I didn't examine this misalignment that my friend had exposed? Sure, I can point back to many hand-me-down stories that help to shape my thinking about what to share, when to share and how to share…but it is all rather pointless. Because once I was shown this truth that had been living in the "space between" I couldn't simply look away without changing my underlying values and beliefs about who I really was.

Unbeknownst to her, she had handed me my permission slip. I took it from her gently not knowing exactly what it meant, only sensing it was the time to put down the shield and expose my brave heart.

I wish I could tell you that this was a one and done experience…that once you've been handed and accept your permission slip to unzip that you are never faced with needing to be brave again in the same way, but that wouldn't be the truth. We are constantly being tested to varying degrees in our lives as leaders. The question is: Will we choose to publicly opt-in and unzip further as we fearless face our fears of further exposing ourselves to the heat or chill that fills the room, or will we choose to privately opt-out where we remain in the stands but longingly yearn to be in the arena where the action is?

Walking the Fine Line

There's a fine line between excitement and fear, danger and safety, comfort and discomfort. At any given moment we are invited to tip toe along the edge of the line without even knowing it. Gracefully ebbing and flowing in and out of integrity with oneself as a way of making peace with the direction a leader or leaders are taking the organization. Navigating the barriers, twists, turns and rocky paths is often tricky. These are the moments that have the ability to be transformative, if we allow it.

Yet it isn't the event itself that transforms, it is the way we relate to and deal with this "intense, often traumatic, always unplanned experience" that informs and ultimately become "the sources of [our] distinctive leadership abilities." Warren Bennis and Robert Thomas, in their 2002 *Harvard Business Review* article "Crucibles of Leadership" define this transformative experience as a crucible. They go on to say that "crucibles force leaders into deep self-reflection," where they actively challenge their beliefs and assumptions and revisit core values. Ultimately, this alters how they relate to life, living, others as well as themselves. Bennis and Thomas had this to say about the leaders they interviewed: "Invariably, they emerged from the crucible stronger and more sure of themselves and their purpose—changed in some fundamental way."

If you've experienced a moment such as this, you know firsthand this isn't for the faint of heart. It will shake you to your core, just as it did for me.

As I approached the end of my term as Chair-elect, I found myself facing personal and professional challenges with how current leadership was addressing matters of significance.

Once again, I found myself questioning my own integrity and that of my leadership. I didn't notice this reflection immediately as I had conveniently allowed myself to become swept up in the rapids of the thoughts and feelings of other prevailing leaders who I believed had more authority and power than I perceived myself as having at the time. And frankly, it was much more comfortable to just sit silently in the stands, giving them the impression that I agreed with their opinion on the best way to handle the dilemma, than it was to face my own fear and stand up in courage. To do so would mean I would have to address my truth, unzip and cross the line.

Now, I know what you are thinking…I did it. I stopped hiding and found the courage to walk the fine line…damn, even cross the line. Well, no, that isn't how the rest of this story goes.

The months that followed were extremely difficult. Hiding in the shadows of my own mind, not sharing with anyone my true thoughts and feelings about how things were unfolding. And what's interesting is this wasn't the only place that I was having this experience. I was faced with similar challenges at work and with my ailing parents who lived 600 miles away. Feeling like I was living in the Twilight Zone with parallel dimensions swirling and intersecting simultaneously with no escape was beyond overwhelming. I couldn't find the "space between" to discover a way forward. Everything was dark. I needed someone or something to illuminate what I couldn't see but I wasn't someone who was practiced at asking for help. Instead, as the overwhelm rose, I found myself wanting to quit everything. I recall numerous times curling up in the farthest corner of my closet contemplating what I could get rid of in my life that would create freedom.

And then, it happened.

As I was leaving a transition meeting to head back home my phone rang and it was the group that I had just been meeting with. As one of them spoke, I found myself in disbelief of what they were saying. I vividly recall becoming viscerally ill and my eyesight blurry. I had stopped listening entirely as I made the decision to just keep driving, just wanting to be home. Nothing made sense. I couldn't do or participate in what was about to happen later that evening. I didn't know what to do on top of everything else I had to do.

I curled up in a fetal position on my bed, staring out the window at the crisp blue sky. A bird singing that Spring had arrived could be heard but it felt more like the darkness of Winter to me. I closed my eyes tightly shutting out the world as I looked inward for the answer. Several hours later, my now ex-husband arrived home and touched me lightly on the shoulder to make sure I was awake given the time. It was then, I cracked. My zipper busted wide open revealing a broken spirit, heart and mind.

I directed him to call the organization and tender my immediate resignation as Chair-elect. As he did so, I never imagined that just a few short days later and after many conversations, I would be standing humbly in front of the board followed by membership completely unzipped in the middle of the arena where the critics were ready to take their blows. The "space between" had appeared as I stood there despite my fears to account for my actions. The board asked me to reconsider and return to lead the organization as Chair. I knew to do so meant I would have to stand on the edge and share, without attributing blame, requesting permission to unzip and asking them to do the same so trust could be regained.

Any time we are abruptly thrown off course, it is an opportunity to reexamine our lives, our values, and where we are headed.

– Judy Lief, "Welcome to the Real World"

The months, and even years, that followed were filled with an ongoing examination of "who did I want to be as a leader?" Let me be clear, I wasn't in search of particular leader or even leadership style to emulate, no, instead this crucible experience had illuminated the next step in my leadership journey; a path that led me to develop my own personal vision for what I wanted from life and define the person I wanted to be as I lived my life. At the time, I didn't have a framework to follow, so I listened intently to my intuition that repeatedly encouraged me to ruminate on this very question, "Who did I want to be?" As I gained confidence, I began sharing my thoughts with trusted friends who helped me eventually make the intangible tangible and who continue to offer support as I inch closer toward realizing my dream.

It was only in writing this book that I discovered the work of Richard Boyatzis, a professor in the Departments of Organizational Behavior and Psychology at Case Western Reserve and a visiting professor of Human Resources at ESADE in Barcelona. In the summer of 2006, he and Annie McKee authored an article for the *Journal of Organizational Excellence* called "Intentional Change" where they used Boyatzis' *Intentional Change Theory* as the primary construct. Interestingly, the first discovery of five that he identified as necessary for sustainable personal change is labeled as the *ideal self.* This initial step is where you define "what you want out of life and the person you want to be—leading to your personal vision."

Remarkably, this model succinctly maps my own leadership journey following my crucible experience.

Here's the good news: Boyatzis didn't develop this theory in response to life-altering crucible events or what complexity theory calls "emergence." He and McKee recognized that part of the challenge of creating and "sustaining excellent leadership is to recognize, manage, and even direct one's own process of learning and change. People who manage their own development intentionally are poised to make good choices about what they need to do to be more effective and more satisfied with their lives." The Intentional Change Model, therefore, was designed to help people mindfully engage in their own personal transformation. In other words, it gives leaders the clear path toward accepting their permission slip to unzip and remain unzipped.

I Am Here, Here I Am

We will know we are living in integrity when we can silence the distractions around and within us while simultaneously sensing a deep resonance that confirms what our brave heart already knows: Our internal compass is now pointing True North instead of wavering off course toward someone else's star.

As we embrace our integrity—the truth of who we are, how we are, why we are—like that of someone we are madly in love with and adore, we experience a heightened level of self-trust. A new level of confidence in our competency, reliability, sincerity and care to take care of what we care most about. Our integrity amplifies our executive presence that carries with it the human truth of oneness with oneself: I Am Here, Here I Am. Here the ego is quieted and only the truest essence of the leader that we are is revealed.

Self-trust produces a resilient state of mind where we believe no matter what comes our way, we will be able to handle it. Building self-trust is a non-trivial, ever evolving step on our journey to live and lead with integrity.

Our relationship with ourselves is the most important relationship we can develop. And just like with all relationships, it takes time, effort and good communication. Without good communication with ourselves, we take an enormous risk and leave ourselves wide open to the possibility that our perceptions about self and others will become distorted.

Exploring the *Space Between*: A Moment of Pause

Begin your Executive Reflection by inviting stillness. Find a still point between your thoughts by bringing your attention to your breath. Sit quietly as you consider how your own integrity has been tested.

Take some time to write your leadership crucible story.

Capturing the details.

Paying close attention to how this experience has played a role in evolving your self-trust.

In 1870, Ralph Waldo Emerson wrote in his essay *Success* that *"Self-trust is the first secret of success."* I couldn't agree more. As you consider ways to develop your self-trust, I encourage you to begin by:

Keeping Promises to Yourself. It's easy to put others ahead of ourselves while disregarding the promises we've made to ourselves. Every time we do, we erode the relationship we are building with ourselves. Do you trust yourself to keep promises you make to yourself? If you answer no, then how can you expect to trust anyone else? Furthermore, do you respect those you can't trust? Of course not. And if you don't trust yourself, you don't respect yourself. How can you then ask others to respect you if you don't respect yourself first?

Speaking to Yourself with Kindness. Turn your inner critic into a nurturing one. Notice what you are saying to yourself throughout the day. How does this chatter influence your experience of yourself and those around you? Turn this negative chatter into your personal Care Committee.

Avoiding People Who Purposefully Erode Your Self-Trust. Although you can't avoid all the naysayers in your life, you can be choiceful with whom you surround yourself with. How are those around you supporting you and your dreams? If they are not, then make decisions on how much time you are willing to invest with them.

Chapter Five
Shatter the Illusion

Do you really know how you are perceived by others? Is it possible that you are simply an emperor with no clothes and no one is telling you? How do you know for sure that how you see yourself is as how others experience you?

These are daunting questions that are fraught with uncertainty and confusion.

These questions challenge a general belief most of us have about ourselves: We are an open book and what we intend is what people see and experience. Yet the truth is that there is often a wide "space between" our intent and the impact that creates this invisible deception that radically informs our leadership, shaping how we lead and ultimately how it defines our personal identity and brand. If the fallacy goes undetected, the cost may be too high to recover from, resulting in career limiting or career ending outcomes. It is why this illusion, known by psychologists as the *illusion of transparency*, must be understood and shattered in order for us to live and lead with integrity.

This is not a rare phenomenon. The illusion arises when we overestimate our ability to easily convey our emotions and thoughts to others. And as a result, we overestimate our ability to understand the emotions and thoughts of others. We believe we know others better than they know us.

"Listen Angela, I am 100% clear all the time. I take great pride in my ability to present information in a clear and concise way. That is what is so baffling. There is absolutely no way my team can misunderstand anything I am telling them to do. It has gotten to the point of frustration. We are behind on our performance goals; leaving me to conclude that no one, besides myself, is taking this situation seriously. I am unsure what this team was doing before I arrived, but what I can tell you is what they are not doing today. They are not following my lead. They are not being clear with their teams on how to improve performance. You know Angela, that's who you need to work with. You can help me by working with my team on improving *their* ability to communicate clearly."

This is a snippet of an initial executive coaching conversation with a client who had been hired to run a significant portion of a newly reorganized company. Further conversation revealed that he had anchored himself to the belief that his communication was clear 100% of the time and there was no possible way for others to misunderstand or misread him. As he said, "I am a see what you get kinda guy." His inability to recognize his love affair with his self-imposed self-image of being clear, limited his ability to recognize that true clarity arises from our acute skill to listen attentively for what is both understood and delicately present in the "space between." The illusion of transparency is stealth. It sneaks up on us in the middle of the night, clouding our ability to lead effectively.

This is not an unusual story. I frequently see this in my work with executives. Leaders ascend to the C-Suite believing they have arrived. In arriving at their much sought-after destination, their egocentric bias emerges, blinding them to the way they are perceived by others. This self-indulgence leads to their peers and teams working around them instead of alongside.

Who Is Looking in the Funhouse Mirror?

The county fair is where the carnies set up the carnival rides and where I had my first encounter with funhouse mirrors. I am unsure why anyone thought these mirrors were "fun" or even funny. When I peered into the mirror, the image that shot back at me was distorted almost beyond recognition. My neck stretched to the length of a giraffe, my body resembled a hippopotamus and I stood two feet tall. There was nothing attractive about the image that fearfully looked back at me. And certainly not funny. I couldn't stand looking at myself this way. My image was distorted by the multitudes of waves embedded in the mirror. I didn't see myself the way my reflection bounced back at me. Instead of being curious, I looked away wishing I hadn't looked to begin with.

In 2014, Suzaan Oltmann, an independent distributor at one of South Africa's FET Colleges, defined the three elements of self-image.

The first is the way a person *perceives or thinks* of him/herself.

The second dimension speaks to the way a person *interprets* others' perceptions—or what he/she thinks the other thinks—of him/herself

And the third, is defined as "the way a person *would like to be* or his/her *ideal self.*"

She further defines the six dimensions of our self-image:

1. **Physical dimension:** How a person evaluates his or her appearance.
2. **Psychological dimension:** How a person evaluates his or her personality.
3. **Intellectual dimension:** How a person evaluates his or her intelligence.
4. **Skills dimension:** How a person evaluates his or her social and technical skills.
5. **Moral dimension:** How a person evaluates his or her values and principles.
6. **Sexual dimension:** How a person feels he or she fits into society's masculine/feminine norms.

The three elements work within each of the six dimensions creating a kaleidoscopic, multifaceted self-image that is ever evolving. For example, as an executive leader, I may see myself and also believe that others agree that I have superior intelligence and are more skillful than most. In my mind, I conclude that my ideal self is already the real self and that is good enough. "By 'real'," as described by Richard Boyatzis, I mean "the person that other people see and with whom they interact." I worked with a CEO who held firmly to this very self-image. He loved who he thought himself to be and believed others admired it too. After two-years, he thanked me for showing him where his staff was underdeveloped in their thinking. The illusion remained firmly intact.

As you can see from this example, the self-image we have of ourselves informs the actions we take, how we take action on those actions with, to, and/or alongside others. If our self-image and our personal experience others have of us are misaligned, we have a self-image-brand identity conflict.

The important thing to remember is that all of this is self-imposed.

It's our own reflection of ourselves about ourselves. We become the subject of our own scrutiny or praise as if we are someone that is separate from ourselves. If we are not careful, our mind and eyes play tricks on us and we only see ourselves as reflected in the mirror. Our self-image, when over or under inflated, erodes our ability to lead in integrity. Once we are out of integrity within ourselves, the challenge intensifies, making it impossible for our self-image to align with the experience others are having of us and thus our leadership brand is on the line.

S.O.S.

In working with C-Suite executive leaders individually and as a team, I am privileged with the opportunity to see and listen into the "space between." Here is where the subtle but growing signs of distress first appear. The distress, if you are unaware of where or how to look for the warning signs, is cloaked in laughter, and tongue and cheek responses, faint and almost inaudible at times. Leaders don't often ask for help immediately. Some never do. They stay keenly focused on their own part of the organization in hopes the other parts will stay afloat without their need to get involved in the rescue. It is of course always someone else's problem. But with frustration rising and a fear that the ship might capsize, the S.O.S. signal always comes in the form of a question.

"So tell me. What do I do about the COO? I don't trust her. I am not even sure what she does. And it strikes me that she is protected. She doesn't do anything she says she is going to do. It is creating big problems for me, my peers and my directs. What suggestions do you have?"

"I don't have any suggestions," I replied. And then comes the silence followed by the eye roll and the rhetorical question, "What do we pay you for?"

"This," I replied.

The back and forth persists until which time the executive inevitably makes the first move suggesting that I am suggesting he should say something to the COO. Remaining completely still, I look squarely into the eyes of the executive and invite him to see into the "space between" us. "Yes, I would want someone to tell me if I were showing up this way, but I am not sure I am the one to do it. It feels risky. And besides, this is the job for the CEO, not me."

A slow reply arises, "Really, what makes you say that?"

"It feels dangerous to me," replies the executive.

"And if you didn't experience it as dangerous?"

"Ok…ok. I see where you are pointing my attention. I need to decide the best way to approach her so she doesn't feel attacked."

This conversation went on for several more conversations. The result was the COO rationalized and even discounted what not only this executive but members of the executive team offered her until which time the team

90

no longer believed anything they had to say would make a positive difference. When the COO looked in the mirror, she saw someone who was reliable, trustworthy, hardworking and getting a lot done. What her peers experienced was someone who was unreliable, untrustworthy, hardworking but getting nothing done because she was too far in the weeds. The gap grew as work arounds commenced.

When our colleagues get to a point that they are unwilling to share their experiences to help us true up our own self-image or if their many attempts have been disregarded, then we can be assured they are standing behind us, peering over our shoulder sympathetically laughing at the image they see. A distorted view of our perceived self-truth keeps us from evolving. Further misinforming our overall view of who we are in relationship with others.

In this case, the lack of integrity between the COO's self-image and her brand identity cost her a significant opportunity to expand her scope. Distraught, she eventually left the company. She was unable to see what others were telling her. "I can't get my head around what they are saying," she'd often say. If only she could have imagined herself in the way that was described. Giving serious consideration to the perspectives of others opens new possibilities for how we see ourselves. If the COO had been willing to listen and look with curiosity, she may still be in the seat.

Straightening the Wave

Gaining insight into how others experience us while acknowledging our own interpretation of ourselves, enlarges our field of awareness. Straightening the wave means we must prepare ourselves to confront possible painful insights and difficult feedback that comes from asking for others' perspectives on who we are for them, how we are experienced in comparison to our own self-image. Despite our fears, we take a courageous posture and invite others to allow us to see ourselves through their lens. We bravely fend off our initial and internal reactions of justifications such as defensiveness, righteousness, blame, shame and/or guilt as a way to remain protected. Instead of continuing on our solo and siloed self-enhancement journey to nowhere, we invite others to reflect back our image so we can live and lead in integrity.

It's scary stuff. Our egos love us as we are, so asking doesn't come naturally. What does come naturally is staying as we are and continuing our blind belief that we are as we see ourselves in the mirror. More often than not, this is the case...until things get out of whack in our relationships with others when we are forced to look at ourselves in new ways, especially when we value remaining on the team.

Straightening the wave requires us to apply our own heat while tugging and testing our own assumptions. This begins by first reflecting and then authoring our own self-assessment. A process of looking at yourself in order to assess aspects that are important to your identity. This work is not an event or a one and done exercise. It can be completed alone, or you may choose to engage a coach or learning partner to support you in the process. This self-assessment may take the shape of a linear process or be more kindred to a mind map. Whatever the form, the self-assessment encompasses your why or purpose, your what you do to fulfill your purpose, and most importantly the behaviors and actions you engage as you fulfill your intended purpose.

This is where things get interesting.

If you are noticing that you don't know where to begin and this feels overwhelming, begin with a guided self-exploration, one that will not only provide possible insights into your interests and possible places to explore where your passions may lie but also reveals hidden insights into the hidden expectations that you have of the world and those in it. Yes, there is one instrument that I am aware of that provides this level of intimate insight, if taken honestly. This personality instrument, The Birkman Method® is a great starting point to begin looking at oneself using data that meets the rigorous standards of validity and reliability. It is a tool that I have introduced to several hundreds of leaders and their teams since becoming a certified consultant in 2005. It's been a game changer every single time.

I vividly remember the day in 2005 when I got my own results. A hot steamy summer afternoon in Camden, South Carolina. The air was thick, no breeze and after a two-hour break it was my turn to have my report read by one of the most experienced senior consultants, who, by the way, was a dear friend and colleague of the assessment's creator, Dr. Roger Birkman. It was rare opportunity to gain learning and insights so close to the actual source.

As I walked with purpose, as I often did, from the bed and breakfast where I was staying to the location where the conference was being held, the sweat dripping down my back and brow, I noticed anxiety arising in me. What if this instrument told me something I didn't like? What if it told me who I believed I was? I felt pretty certain I had mastered the art of self-awareness…so really, I thought, what in the world is the fear and worry all about. Well, if you knew the instructor of this course, it may have been clearer. She was accurate, direct, knowledgeable, expert and less than compassionate as a teacher and after the morning session with her, I realized I had every right to be concerned for how I might receive anything she had to share. She would be right. The instrument would be right. And where would that leave me?

Where did that leave me…? Shocked. As she read the report to me, explaining every detail, I soon realized I was barely listening to what she had to say. I felt queasy and disoriented as the sweat intensified even though I was now sitting in an air-conditioned space. Sure, it was a hot, humid and steamy afternoon in Camden, South Carolina, but believe me the intensity grew within me as the voices in my head kept screaming, "This is utterly wrong. This cannot be my report. And who, on God's earth, was this senior consultant referencing as she spoke? Surely it wasn't me. I didn't resemble any of what she said the report reported, except of course, the good stuff." You know what I am talking about. The good stuff being what I liked about myself plus the affirmation I had previously received over my lifetime from others. The kind of things that made me stand up a bit taller, with my shoulders back and my chin held high.

Yup, there was a lot that was revealed that I didn't appreciate or even like. I remember sitting in complete and utter silence, alone with only the voices in my head—which were screaming at me. The trance was broken when the senior consultant eagerly asked, "So, what do you think?" I just shook my head side to side as I stood up from the small square table. I reluctantly picked up the report that had inaccuracies and shoved it in my backpack, saying nothing except thank you and good-bye. I was speechless.

The remainder of the afternoon and evening, I challenged myself to see myself as the report and described. It was painful to question what I had always thought I knew. And yet, I was now faced to look in the mirror with data in hand that came only from me. This was when my wave began to straighten out.

Not everyone's wave begins the process of straightening the way mine did. In fact, in all the Birkman reports I've delivered, I have yet to find one, not one person, who has had this experience as I read their reports. Maybe that's because I share my story and report openly with everyone I work with. I reveal it all and point out where I still struggle, where and how I've grown, noting the discipline and practice I intentionally invested to become a better human being. Maybe that eases their minds and opens them to laugh instead of hearing the defensive voices that keep us hostage, remaining blind to our wavy reflection in the mirror.

Ironing Out the Wrinkle

Often our own ironing is enough to begin the process of flattening the wave in the funhouse mirror. Other times, it takes a bit more to release the grip of our deeply embedded and persistently held constructed beliefs that we have of ourselves, the world and how we engage within it. We look at the iron and notice the setting is actually on silk and not linen. We choose to turn up the heat. We grab the starch and fill the reservoir with water. Now we are ready…or are we?

I am not sure we can ever be ready, really ready that is, to invite and receive 360° feedback. It's a gutsy move to turn up the heat when we really don't know what temperature we can actually stand without being scorched. It's why, I believe, more often than not, we just leave the wrinkle where it is at.

It's a perfectly perfect conclusion to leave well enough alone.

The waves aren't that big anyway, right?

We convince ourselves that no one probably even notices or even cares anyway.

As much as we say we are curious about what others' think, the truth is that we would actually prefer to think that we already know how they think than to check it out for ourselves. It's easier to leave the wrinkle; holding onto the hope no one notices, thus saving the effort to straighten it out. Yet for those like me, who can't stand wrinkles and waves, this means we have no choice but to engage in a formal feedback loop. In making this choice, we understand that bravery is a prerequisite to entering the "space between." Our bravery enables us to walk the fine line between what we know, and what we think we know in order to see ourselves as others see us. We know that the heat invites the insights that have been missing and it possesses the power to shift our perspective; moving us to make different choices for how we can live and lead with integrity.

When we do this, we stand in the center of the arena as Brené Brown would say. We ask the "others" to generously spray their starch—their assessments, experiences and perspectives—with compassion, courage and candor onto the wrinkles we do not see while we remain receptive to receiving the insights that arise from the heat.

Like ironing, the preparation and setup are the most important. Inviting the right mix and cross-section of people into the conversation matters. How you express why they were chosen matters. And any and all asks you to make them matter. It all matters. To get the wrinkles out of delicate material takes finesse, gentleness and care. We are all delicate. We are human even if we proclaim a thick, rough exterior.

Although there are many varieties and ways to conduct a 360° it is important to choose the one that best aligns with your cares. Each has their benefits. Regardless of the form, it's very important to remember what we are doing; namely, inviting the listeners of who we are to become the speakers for the sake of shattering the illusions we have been living.

Who Is This Staring Back at "Me"? It Is "I"?

Data is useful only when we choose to do something with it.

It is true that inaction is a form of action. We've come to know this as complacency. Complacency is nothing more than half-hearted attempts at doing something which in my opinion, does not count at all as action.

Doing something does mean taking committed action based on the data obtained from our self-assessments, evaluations and reflections. It's this very data plus the corresponding actions that help us to rid ourselves of the fun house mirror that's been hanging on our interior hallway walls for way too long. With committed action, we get clear that it is time to replace this mirror with a new one; one that truly reflects our inner truth outwardly while consistently matching the impressions others have of us.

Yes, it's a daunting task to replace the mirror. It is often extremely heavy. And it may require the wall be repainted where it once hung. If we are not careful, we will come up with a million reasons to stare into the same mirror instead of replacing it.

The key is to embrace the feedback as data, points of consideration, and without stumbling upon the emotional landmines that lay all around. I realize what I am asking is extremely challenging and not possible 100% of the time. If we do not push forward and embrace the feedback as mere data points, we will find ourselves seeking escape, standing in front the familiar mirror, placing blame, giving reasons why while making excuses in order to have the feedback make sense...and yet, it is this very move that keeps us stuck in the illusion, where our internal brand and external brand do not align. A trick played on us by our minds.

Our deceptive minds will betray us. Our minds will mask this betrayal with feelings and thoughts that conflate the truth. Our minds will do its best to convince us that it is actually others who have betrayed us. Our minds do this to make sense. Our bodies do it to elude the discomfort of dissonance we feel; the unsteadiness and discomfort that comes from the wave being straightened.

When we choose committed action, in the form of an action learning development plan, we at first feel awkward and we look funny even to ourselves. The gaps, strengths and areas of opportunity present themselves in ways that are unfamiliar, and our experience is likely one of uncertainty. And that is ok. It is to be expected. You are not alone. Many have had similar experiences to varying degrees.

When synthesizing your data into a usable action learning development plan, I find it helpful to engage a coach or a mentor as a thought-partner, advisor, accountability partner, and creative muse to help tease out the parts that seem complicated, unnecessary, or in leftfield. An objective partner enables us to see when we are nearing thresholds so we can feverishly prepare and check that our integrity is fully intact.

Exploring the *Space Between*: Sparks Fly

It takes bravery and courage to look at ourselves through the lens of others. To do so requires us to push past our desire to continue on our own journey of self-enhancement without concern for how we are outwardly perceived. We are beings of connection: Connection to ourselves, to others and to the world. Connection is necessary to live in and lead with integrity.

As we inch even closer to realizing the power and fullness of our own integrity—where our internal self matches the expressions provided by our external self as evidenced by experiences of others—we come to experience a deeply profound sensation, one that may be new or one that may be familiar, regardless if it is unexpected. I refer to this as a "sparks fly." The precious moment when new insights and inspirations come without warning simply because we are living our inner truth out loud. When we embark on this journey, sparks are always flying. We can see the sparks fly as if for the first time, yet, they have been there all along, waiting for us in the "space between."

Now, let's pause on our journey. Inhale deeply through your nose noticing the cool air. Hold your breath at the top for a moment and then slowly release it through the nose. Notice the warm as the breath leaves your body. For a moment, when you are empty of breath, again pause. This four-part breathing practice relaxes the mind and body giving way to even more deep awareness. Once you feel settled, here is your moment of executive reflection:

- Now that you have a new awareness to see your own illusions, what name will you give them? By naming them we demystify them.
- What have you been doing in a half-hearted way?
- What steps do you need to take to move toward action?
- What is holding you back?

Chapter Six
The Intersection

Integrity arises most easily when, after a long journey down some unfamiliar and windy path, we become increasingly curious and interested in "what is" versus "what isn't." Our conversation with ourselves and others changes. We begin to consider: "What is possible here?" "Where might this take me if I let go of how I believe it could or should be?" "I wonder if being in this position or situation is actually pointing me somewhere else?" "What have I been overlooking?"

As we continue our self-discovery journey to live in and lead from integrity, we find ourselves on the same unfamiliar and windy path, yet suddenly it looks wildly different than before. We might even argue that it is a different path entirely.

I promise you it isn't.

The path we are on is the path that we are on. It only looks different because we are different. We now see things that we previously overlooked before. We appreciate our past and present moments for what they are, not what they are not. And we acknowledge that we are the creators of our future by the choices and actions that we take in this present moment.

Being creators means we acknowledge our own creativity. And in doing so, what wasn't clear before, now becomes clear. As the fog lifts, we see further ahead and notice the next gentle bend in the road. One that we'd swear wasn't there just moments before.

With our interest peaked, we pause for just a moment, dropping all the baggage we've been carrying. As we kneel to pick it up, we decide the load is simply too heavy. We carefully begin the sorting process, selecting only what we need, leaving the rest behind. The lightness allows us to move more quickly toward what lies ahead.

And we continue.

We approach the bend peering around the corner ahead.

We see in the distance a crossroads of sorts. A lovely surprise as we've been on this path for what seems to be a very long time. From a distance, this intersection feels foreign, and yet it also seems vaguely familiar.

As we make our approach, we begin to realize that this intersection is the precise one we've been searching for. Yet it was in the trusting, not the active searching that it appeared.

The discomfort of asking new questions and owning our choices is the trusting I'm referring to. Continuously pushing ourselves outside our prescribed comfort zone. It is here, we make the realization that this indeed is where life begins; beyond the boundaries we had set or those that had been set for us. With the boundaries removed, anything is possible; our life is possible. In this moment, our old path appears new, and we reimagine it with fresh eyes, unsure where it will lead. All we know is we must take a few steps forward on the path each day and be open to meeting our Self there.

It is true that some are fortunate to stumble upon this path early in life. Others, like me, discover it mid-way through. And then there are the others who finally say, "what the hell" and take off running down the path where their purpose and passion intersect. They are the ones who have known where the intersection was all along, but the "busyiness," the doingness, and the rightness of life were distractors. Life for them, as it was for me for way too long, became an either/or, not a both/and. This scenario is true for many. We choose not to move toward our intersection, possibly out of necessity, or our desire to meet the expectations others have for us, or a thousand other reasons; we choose without really feeling like choice is an option. We feel stuck.

Pushing our gifts aside means we are not living in nor can we effectively lead from our and with integrity. Why? Because we are seeking something that isn't available. Promotions, spans of control, higher levels of authority, prestige and recognition satisfy us only for a moment…and then the inevitable returns.

Overwhelm, frustration, shame, blame, guilt, resignation, resentment, keeps us small. To avoid the tension that is alive inside us, we pacify ourselves by convincing our hearts that one day we will pursue our dreams.

But does this really happen? Does waiting pay off?

The risk is too high for me. Waiting is not an option.

Nor should it be for you.

Patience on the other hand is a requirement. Waiting and patience are two very different things. Waiting to have enough or be enough is very different than being patient in our own development toward our own intersection.

Stop the Waiting Game

Life is not a passive sport. It's an active one. One of preparation, speculation, and acting in real time toward our intersection. We are living life creatively, not waiting for life to happen. We experience ourselves as resourceful, complete, and whole as we are. We accept we are perfectly imperfect and share this type of perfection with the world unapologetically. We step forward and practice new things repeatedly until they become habits. We change these habits when they are no longer of value in our quest. We are constantly evolving. We are not waiting for the best part of our life to arrive.

Waiting was the game of my parents. It was the game of my grandparents. I am guessing it was the game of a long line of my ancestors. Was waiting the context you grew up in? My hunch is yes. My assessment arises from my work where far too many say to me, "I just need to put in the hours now, so later I take some time needed for myself."

And this narrative occurs year after year after year until we become seduced by the comfort of doing more, making the waiting less noticeable. Secretly hoping it will be worth the wait.

My parents waited. And they waited and waited and waited.

There was always something, however, that couldn't wait. "Doing" couldn't wait. There was always something to do and it needed doing right now. The list never got shorter. Their exhaustion only got longer to the point they couldn't recover. Sleep was an evil necessity for the more doing that was necessary.

Notice I didn't use the word rest.

Sleep isn't rest and rest doesn't mean sleep.

My mother never rested, although she slept. She always thought about the million things there were to do, counting and recounting them in her head over and over for lest she might forget. It was common to find her mopping the kitchen floor at 2:30am. Doing became her life. Doing controlled her, she didn't control it. If the world was lucky enough to still have her here, she would tell us to, "Stop the doing. Stop the waiting. This is not life. Life is a purpose filled doing and doing it with your entire heart because you love it." She knew this even as she did more, waiting for the moment she could live. That moment never arrived. It makes me incredibly sad to realize she lived a life not in integrity even though she was honorable, a woman who kept her word, and someone who believed deeply in the universal promise of salvation on earth. She suffered unnecessarily. Doing it will do that to you if you play the waiting game.

This was real for me. As I'm reminded of, "The apple doesn't fall far from the tree."

As is the case for many, I spent way too long on the path of "doing." Doing more. Doing more to do more in search of something. Maybe my purpose. Maybe my passion. Maybe, simply and mostly likely, to please my parents.

This approach to life, however, turned on me in the most radical and unexpected way.

By the time I was thirty-eight, I was considered by many as professionally successful: A senior vice president who possessed enormous influence inside a 30,000-person organization. I was unanimously granted the authority to coach and work with presidents and their teams in strategically shifting the trajectory of their performance. It was a wildly exciting time. We were on top of our game more often than not. I loved being on the field working with executive teams. The impact was noticeable, and it mattered. I mattered. I believed that my innate ability of doing more, more often and doing it better than anyone else was the reason why. So, I kept doing it until I couldn't do it anymore. I was faced with a significant physical breakdown.

Life called a "time out."

What the hell is a "time out" and who in the hell has time for a "time out" I thought. No one. I was pissed. So, for four more years, I suffered and pushed harder. Pressing forward day after day was the only way I knew to perform in my pursuit of reducing the pressures I faced as a professional and as a member of the so-called "sandwich generation." This unfriendly, twisted road backtracked upon itself repeatedly until I finally found myself physically exhausted with no medical explanation of why. I had no choice but to stop at the stop sign and look up.

In my mid-forties, I stopped doing it for the sake of doing more and being applauded for it. I realized it wasn't the medal I wanted to pursue any longer. The shininess has faded, replaced with countless hours of emptiness.

In its place, I chose to stop and take stock. Repacking my bag. I accounted for what I had been carrying, discarding what wasn't mine, offering the gifts of unspoken expectations back to those that had placed them in my bag.

That magical moment when I bravely peered into and stood firmly in the threshold of my life, was the very moment my life changed. Doing wasn't the answer. It had never been the answer. I turned away from doing and toward experiencing.

It's then that I experienced a most unexpected surprise that comes from experiencing an experience in real time. I became intimately aware of the learning that had always been present but I had ignored. Living life in this way was "like" rocket science. Yet in my busyness of doing more faster, I lived as if it wasn't. In fact, I could often be overheard saying energetically, "This isn't rocket science people. Just stay focused and do it." How wrong I was.

Standing in the Intersection

This is when my purpose magically found me.

A more accurate and truer statement is: This is when I first became aware my purpose actually existed. It had been with me all along; poking me in the back, tapping me on the shoulder, begging me to slow down long enough to listen and take notice. And in my busyness of doing, I was blind to its presence. I was consumed with the feelings of pridefulness of my doing and accomplishing and checking things off the list. My purpose, I believed if I were lucky, would be discovered in my busyness of doing.

Instead, what I discovered standing in the intersection of purpose and passion was profound. An inflection point appeared along with the realization that being masterful at the art of busily doing was nothing more than a cover-up successfully achieved by my con artists, those who I know as our inner critics. Their mission is a simple one: Relentless hold firmly to the beliefs I'd been swimming in since birth.

I suddenly felt scared. Knee knocking scared. What if I drown here? Where is my life preserver? The pool I'd have to swim in looked dark and unfriendly. I couldn't imagine what might be lurking in this "space between." I had to make a choice: Look squarely into the eyes of the unknown or retreat and return to the comfort of my old ways.

Being a martyr wasn't my destiny, so I chose to stand in, not at, the intersection of my truth. Staring directly into the "space between" where I witnessed "what was, is now, and is becoming" all in the same precise moment. The kaleidoscope of possibilities danced vividly in front of and in me. The unfolding of my future was breathtaking if only I was willing to forsake the busyness of doing and begin the arduous practice of becoming skillful in the art of experiencing experiences and then reflecting on the reflection of these experiences. This meta-level view affords the ability to move from the "Me-view" where I worry about being good enough, smart enough, loveable enough to the "I-view" that is not dependent on self-worth and doesn't need external validation. It is here where I met, for the first time, my creative inspirations, insights, and innovations for living life fully immersed.

Inside the Matrix, I discovered what was truly required of me, or of anyone, who stands in the face of discomfort, uncertainty, and fear associated with living in and leading with integrity.

Dignity.

Dignity is required to oppose the forces of our tendencies for self-preservation that rumbles deep within our bodies, where the echo of being busy and doing more is championed.

Dignity. A required way of being and leading oneself and being in relationship with others and our world. Congruence of connection at all three intersections is necessary if we wish to realize our fullest potential and be in integrity.

In *Leading with Dignity: How to Create a Culture That Brings Out the Best in People*, Donna Hicks, PhD, author and authority on dignity, points to her discovery of the 10 Elements of Dignity. Here, she challenges us to look deeply at where our dignity may be flourishing and where it may be at risk.

1. **Acceptance of Identity.** Approach people as being neither inferior nor superior to you; give others the freedom to express their authentic selves without fear of being negatively judged; interact without prejudice or bias, accepting that characteristics such as race, religion, gender, class, sexual orientation, age, and disability are at the core of their identities.

2. **Recognition.** Validate others for their talents, hard work, thoughtfulness, and help; be generous with praise; give credit to others for their contributions, ideas, and experience.

3. **Acknowledgement.** Give people your full attention by listening, hearing, validating, and

responding to their concerns and what they have been through.

4. **Inclusion.** Make others feel that they belong, at all levels of relationship (family, community, organization, and nation).

5. **Safety.** Put people at ease at two levels: physically, so they feel free from the possibility of bodily harm, and psychologically, so they feel free from concern about being shamed or humiliated and free to speak up without retribution.

6. **Fairness.** Treat people justly, with equality, and in an evenhanded way, according to agreed-on laws and rules.

7. **Independence.** Empower people to act on their own behalf so that they feel in control of their lives and experience a sense of hope and possibility.

8. **Understanding.** Believe that what others think matters; give them the chance to explain their perspectives and express their points of view; actively listen in order to understand them.

9. **Benefit of the Doubt.** Treat people as if they are trustworthy; start with the premise that others have good motives and are acting with integrity.

10. **Accountability.** Take responsibility for your actions. Apologize if you have violated another person's dignity; make a commitment to change hurtful behaviors.

Dignity opens the door for us to feel our passion as it pulsates through our hearts, souls and bodies while the answer to "why am I here" emerges as if on the big screen in front of us.

Standing in the intersection in this way means we can clearly see the signposts. There's no mistake where we must go or how we are to live and lead from here. We do so in and with integrity, dignity, and grace.

Exploring the *Space Between*: Beyond the Comfort Zone

Amit Ray reminds us, *Magic and mystery lies on the edge, just outside the comfort zone.*

The steps we walk along our journey toward the intersection of our passion and purpose asks us to bravely:

1. **Follow The Clues** that are in view but we cannot readily see.
2. **Fiercely Trust** yourself to turn the kaleidoscope and see the beauty of a new perspective.
3. **Love** going below the speed limit and inviting patience into your life.

Take some time in your Executive Reflection to reflect on the following:

- Where are you dismissing the flashing lights, flood lights, spotlights and neon signs pointing you toward the clues illuminating the direction to walk?
- How has your addiction to being busy and doing faster served you? Are you, like me, sipping

secretly from a discreet paper bag at any chance you get?

- Where are you saying "yes" to the unspoken expectations that others present? Might it be time to give them back generously to those who dropped them at your doorstep so you can receive your own gifts that are wrapped in dignity, grace and integrity?

- If you were to regularly take a moment to pause and reflect, what inspiration might appear that reconnects you to your own creativity?

Chapter Seven
Treasures Hidden Within

So this, I believe, is the central question upon which all creative living hinges: Do you have the courage to bring forth the treasures that are hidden within you?

– Elizabeth Gilbert, Big Magic

The map we've been using as our guide to **Discover the Matrix** is as unique as you are. Each of us takes a different leadership journey in aligning ourselves with the integrity that lies within us. Each of us possess a different set of cares, concerns, limitations, and blind spots that must be addressed. The journey is uniquely ours and the hidden treasures we discover are uniquely ours.

In the 1999 movie, *The Matrix,* Morpheus appears when he believes Neo is ready to not only stop wondering but also stop seeking his truth outside himself. Neo is offered a choice of taking a red pill or blue pill.

As described in the movie by Morpheus, "You take the blue pill…the story ends, you wake up in your bed and believe whatever you want to believe. You take the red pill…you stay in Wonderland, and I show you how deep the rabbit hole goes."

Here within these pages, we too have offered you a choice. The choice to revert to where you remain content in your ignorance, with no memory of what has taken place thus far or continue the practice of untethering yourself by going vertical in your own development where potentially unsettling and life-changing truths will lead you to discover the treasures hidden within.

Choosing the latter is when we are changed forever. We see, understand, and experience the world around us differently. We can honor the trodden path that is now behind us. Our past no longer feels like an anchor to either the best of times or the worst of times.

Instead, we make amends with it all, with a recognition of other choices that were likely available, and we just didn't see them. We reconcile, honor, and move on. We are who we are because of these experiences and now with new discoveries and new information, we choose to be open and present in this moment, noticing the options that are available.

We accept and appreciate that the promise of our life is connected to our ability and willingness to learn, adapt and change. We cannot stop change. Change is a constant state we live in. Yet, if we own our own evolution, we can take full advantage of every opportunity that is presented and experienced leading us toward our center where our superpowers, our treasures, our truths, our integrity reside.

We choose willingly to take the red pill and discover the new discoveries that await us.

Dancing Goats

Do you know the story of how coffee was discovered?

Legend has it that the origin of coffee dates back centuries. It can be traced back to ancient coffee forests on the Ethiopian plateau. There lived a goat herder named Kaldi who made the discovery of coffee after he noticed his goats becoming extremely energetic upon eating berries from a certain tree. They were so energetic in fact that they did not want to sleep at night.

Becoming curious, Kaldi decided to try a few berries for himself. As he bit down, he noticed the outer shell was hard while the softer middle was extremely bitter. Spitting out the morsal, he continued to wonder what it was exactly that made his goats so happy.

On his next trip to a local monastery, Kaldi requested an audience with the abbot. Excited, he shared the berries with him telling him all details of his dancing goats. The abbot told him to stop sharing such gibberish, took the berries from him and threw them harshly into the fire. As Kaldi stood staring into the fire, shame flooded over him. His thoughts were disrupted by popping noises coming from the fire followed by a sweet aroma arising in the air. Once the fire had died out, he carefully raked out what was now the roasted beans, ground them, and placed the powdered substance into a cup of hot water. Coffee was born.

The moral of the dancing goat story:

Be observant about what is happening around you. Suspend judgment for what it is you know or think you know. Engage in curiosity. Ask yourself:

- Where do you see happiness and success around you?
- What might be contributing to this success and happiness?

Remember, when answers seem to not make sense and you find that others dismiss you by casting judgment, don't stop your quest to understand. The best ideas often seem outlandish until they are not.

I often share this story when an executive or entrepreneur or even a team is stuck. Their stuckedness takes the form of "I don't see how we..." or "There's no other way forward that I..." The resignation and resentment and even worry that is present sucks all the air out of the room. To lighten the mood, I share this funny story. It gives them an opportunity to notice how they are looking, from what vantage point they are looking, and what they are looking for. Most often, the look shifts from "being right" to "what might be possible." With curiosity present, we can consider different angles to existing concerns.

Live More Out of Curiosity Than Fear

After several years of being in the workforce, two entrepreneurial women decided to join forces and start their own business. They had a vision for offering a different experience to their clients. Each came into the business with their own preferences for workstyle, approach, and what they enjoyed doing. What one liked to do, the other did not. To them, it seemed like a match made in heaven.

Eight years have passed. The women find themselves wondering where they are and where they are going. The honeymoon was officially over. The questions they had were about direction, growth, and profitability, not about redesigning themselves within the relationship.

I enter stage right.

The scene, for me, was illuminated with bright white spotlights, however, they only experienced darkness, confusion, and bewilderment. The start of our engagement revealed they were struggling both personally and professionally. They were tired and frustrated from the long hours they put in. They didn't say "no" to anyone. And worst of all, they rarely paid themselves for the work they did. They were a company of two doing amazing work for free.

These issues were not a sign of their lack of intelligence. To the contrary, these women were highly intelligent and were masterful at their craft. In their desire to make better designs with better client experiences, they lost sight of themselves and what was important to them. Their integrity was lost in the darkness. Neither spoke openly or honestly about how they were feeling for fear of hurting the other's feelings or worse, fear the business might break up. In their minds, that would be a tragedy. It would mean they'd have to return to working for someone else.

After 9-months in the engagement, and hundreds of hours diving into the way they thought about and ran the business, together we changed how they did things operationally. This ultimately had little impact on results.

Why?

I asked myself that very question. And instead of forcing an answer, I became curious about what it was we, and I, were missing. And then, like a bolt of lightning, it hit me.

They were living and running their business from scarcity, not abundance. They had chosen the blue pill.

No matter what new structures, systems, processes we put in place, fear stole any potential that existed. They could only focus on what might be lost. Fear was strangling them. How then, do I shift their fear to curiosity?

The next time we met, I outlined a creative exercise for them to complete. I asked them to gather up a large sheet of paper, markers, pens, and colored pencils, all of which were accessible to them. I then asked them to draw their vision for their company. I invited them to include as much detail as possible. I encouraged them to leave nothing off their vision boards. To stimulate their creative juices, I asked:

"Where did you see yourself in two years and five years?

What about the business?

What do you want the business (and you) to become known for?

How does this picture inform the role you play in the business?

What else might you like to do that you are not currently doing?

What are you doing that you don't enjoy?"

I gave them 90-minutes to complete the work in total silence. They, in essence, accepted the red pill. What I observed, in real time, was a shift from scarcity to abundance as they made new discoveries about themselves and on another.

As each woman shared their picture and the meaning behind the images, it became apparent to everyone, they had dramatically different hopes and dreams for themselves and for the business. The mood shifted from curiosity and wonderment back to fear. We ended the meeting but not before I acknowledged where we were, inviting them to reflect on the experience and to examine more deeply what each wanted.

Early the next day, I received separate phone calls from both women asking if I'd be willing to meet with them confidentially. I rearranged my day. This simple activity placed them squarely in their "space between" where they couldn't hide from their skeletons, from their real desires, from the need to feel as they did during the one-hour they allowed themselves to swim in possibilities. Each, confidentially, told me they wanted to break up the business. I simply listened and asked them how I might be of assistance in helping them to design the overdue conversation with the other. Within 24-hours, the conversation took place and the unwinding and healing ensued.

Now each one was ready to step fully into their possibilities of designing the future they wanted. They stood in the face of their fears and chose to dance alone creating something different and new.

With their integrity aligned and in hand, they made different discoveries revealing their hidden treasures. This allowed them to step abundantly and bravely into their futures.

Exploring the *Space Between*: A Surprisingly Simple Truth, Trust Your Wings

With our map tightly in hand, we approach the intersection and scan the terrain for where "X" marks the spot, the exact place that signifies where we are to dig. Now that we know there is a hidden treasure within, we are eager to collect all our jewels right now.

I'm with you. I did the same. I hurried up down the path with my map in hand, squeezing it so tightly that the ink where the "X" laid was rubbed off. I closed my eyes to see if I could recall where it had been. I held it up to the light, searching for any residue and found nothing.

I then prayed for a miracle, magic and fairy dust. Still nothing.

I could sense the jewels were within reach, I just couldn't tell where. This time when I closed my eyes, a surprising simple truth was revealed, and I instinctively knew what I needed to do next to find where my treasures were.

I needed to *Trust My Wings*. Tapping into my wisdom, sapience, or sagacity. Trusting our wisdom is innate in our ability to think and act using knowledge, experience, understanding, common sense and insight. It allows for unbiased judgment, compassion, experiential self-knowledge, self-transcendence, and non-attachment and is associated with virtues such as ethics and benevolence.

Yes, this is not only what I needed to do to find my Treasures Hidden Within but it is what we all need to do.

"The Jewel Reflection" exercise taps into our creativity, inviting our wisdom to step forward as we visually describe, using pictures and words, our desired future.

1. At your local hobby or department store, pick up a poster sized frame or you can do a smaller version if you desire. I've also done a Jewel Reflection using software tools such as Adobe Creative on my computer.

2. Collect images that symbolize the experiences, feelings, and things you want to attract into your life.

   I. Use photographs, magazine cutouts, pictures of the Internet that inspire you.
   II. Be creative. Go beyond pictures and include anything that speaks to you. These could be inspirational phrases, words, quotations and thoughts.
   III. Consider including a picture of yourself when you are joyful.

3. Begin placing the special things you've collected on the poster. Arranging and rearranging, inviting your intuition and wisdom to guide you. Be selective. You don't need to use everything you've gathered. Keep it simple. There's elegance and beauty in simplicity and clarity.

Once you feel complete, it is time to step away and reflect on the experience as it unfolded.

- What was it like to experience yourself in this way?
- What was revealed to you as you engaged creatively?

- Which of your strengths or positive aspects of my identity are represented in this future?
- How might I be uniquely equipped to bring this future into reality as a result of what I now see are my unique treasures?
- How can I use these treasures that are represented within the collage more effectively?
- How does this future align with my ideal self?

Once we have our Jewel Reflection, we can refer to it often, contemplating on the choices we are making and whether these choices are using our treasures and gifts in designing our desired future or getting in the way.

Chapter Eight
Dare to Create

Creativity is just connecting things. When you ask creative people how they did something they feel a little guilty because they didn't really do it, they just saw something. It seemed obvious to them after a while. That's because they were able to connect experiences they've had and synthesize new things.

This is a very poignant quote by Steve Jobs that is worth examining a bit closer.

Take a moment to re-read this quote paying particular attention to the parts I've underlined.

<u>Creativity is just connecting things</u>. When you ask creative people how they did something they feel a little guilty because they didn't really do it, <u>they just saw something</u>. It <u>seemed obvious to them after a while</u>. That's because they were <u>able to connect experiences they've had and synthesize new things</u>.

Now, only read the parts I've underlined, allowing the other words to fade into the background.

<u>Creativity is just connecting things</u>. When you ask creative people how they did something they feel a little guilty because they didn't really do it, they <u>just saw something</u>. It <u>seemed obvious to them after a while</u>. That's

because they were <u>able to connect experiences they've had and synthesize new things</u>.

What is revealed when we strip these wise words back to their very essence?

The salient point is this: As human beings, regardless of how we define ourselves, we are always making connections of some kind, and in doing so, we are innately creative and generative.

We are neither stagnant nor permanent.

We are ever changing and evolving with every breath we take, with every new piece of information that is gained, with every choice we make or don't make. Even as you are reading or listening to this, your brain and body are actively and automatically connecting data stored as memories, actively bringing them forward into the present moment in order to understand, curate, innovate, and act. This process is happening unconsciously all the time and so is our creative process. It too is constantly working in the background.

The question is from what mindset is your unconscious working from?

Our minds twist and bend in all kinds of gyrations, constantly seeking and sorting what fits within our limited constructs of knowing and what falls outside it.

Those who stay fixed and firmly rooted in their comfort zone are still creative, they are simply creative in a finite way, contrasting those who do not limit themselves by perceived boundaries and instead embrace the unknown. These generative leaders are courageously creative. They are driven to experiment and explore those connections that lie just outside their comfort zone. They knowingly accept the risk that their ideas may plummet and fail. They faithfully stay the course in pursuit of learning, growth, and discovery of their and the world's infinite possibilities.

Insatiable Appetite

Leaders with a growth mindset are continuously hungry to explore more, experiment more, and experience more. Their learning edge is pushed, tested, and at times cajoled beyond their wildest imagination. There is nothing a generative leader wouldn't do to extend and expand their understanding of the connection they have with themselves, with others, and the world.

If you have ever been around a leader like this, you know just how infectious they are. Everything about them peaks your interests. Your hunger intensifies to be around them. To be on their team would be a dream job.

Who are these radical leaders who move with ease as they double-down their efforts in the face of adversity; see opportunity within challenges; listen attentively to feedback, especially feedback for improvement; consider every angle by seeking out divergent thinking; finds pleasure in the process of practicing their craft called leadership; and finds learning and inspiration in the success of others? These leaders, says Carol Dweck, PhD, and author of *Mindset: The New Psychology of Success,* are those who possess a growth mindset. Her decades of research discovered this simple, yet groundbreaking idea that mindset matters. And those who with a growth mindset as opposed to a fixed mindset "believe their most basic abilities can be developed through their dedication and hard work—brains and talent are just the starting point. This view creates a love of learning and a resilience that is essential for great accomplishment."

From the first time I met this executive, I knew he was special. I wasn't alone in this opinion. I recall both the CEO and President in separate conversations saying, "He's an exciting top hire." I found myself even more intrigued. I wondered what this executive possessed that others may be standing on the verge of.

His introduction had me pause to reflect more deeply on the qualities present in and within the current executive team. I made a list of the individual and team's qualities that I regularly experienced. With a list in hand, I began my engagement with the newest executive and within six-months I began to discover the qualities that were brightly illuminated in him yet were present but dimmer in the others. This discovery didn't take place outside of me, it dropped me into the middle of my own Matrix where I had to ask myself some new questions that helped me evolve and realign my own integrity so I could continue to elevate the executive team.

The Qualities

What I witnessed are the following qualities and principles that may seem fundamental to good leadership, yet, what I've learned over my almost 40 years working in super-sized organizations, with entrepreneurs and business owners, and companies who are positioning themselves to sell is this: Companies of all sizes can be successful without leaders and teams who don't possess these qualities, but those who dare to hire talent and teams who do, watch out.

Peak performance occurs when leaders lead themselves and their teams with integrity. I also discovered they:

1. **Live in and for the moment.** There are no do overs. There is no time for regrets. Every moment is a moment to learn from, be it good or bad (whatever that means).

2. **Dedicate themselves to principled practice.** Having a principled approach to life and leadership creates a working framework to better understand the best way to stay centered in one's well-being while blending in service to others. It requires a deep belief in one's abilities, one's dignity, and one's integrity.

3. **Take chances repeatedly.** Living on the edge takes guts even if there is no glory. Taking calculated risks is energizing. First, you've got to know where your learning edge is and then you need a coach to help you snuggle up against it and cross it bravely.

4. **Embrace change.** Why not? It's happening anyway. The more we hug and fall in love with change the more opportunities that are present. Otherwise, the drift into the "space between," inspirations lost, and we drift into status quo.

5. **Pause to reflect on experiences.** Learning on the fly is only possible when a purposeful pause happens. Otherwise, the new insights trickle between the cracks of the sidewalk and are forever

forgotten, but somehow are repeatedly routinely resulting in frustration instead of ambition.

6. **Ignite the success within others.** Positivity, even when the environment is chaotic and filled with uncertainty, is always present. Positivity isn't an action for faking it until you make it, it's the honesty that comes from speaking your truth with a voice filled with infinite possibilities.

7. **Become the red rubber ball.** Returning to Self to become resourced, replenished, and rejuvenated. Spending time experiencing what you love outside of what you are currently doing, even if you love what you are doing. Pushing the outer edges of what you know and how you learn. Bouncing freely like a red rubber ball means playing and experimenting to reconnect to your source of creative energy.

If you were to lay these qualities next to those identified by Dweck, I know you'd find similarities. This emphasizes the importance of her breakthrough findings. It also demonstrates the power of consistent practice and application. When this is done with rigor there are no limits.

The game, as Simon Sinek has been overheard to say, is infinite.

Beyond the You That Is You

The same can be said of teams and organizations. Those with organizational membership constituted by a growth mindset repeatedly achieve higher levels of performance at every stakeholder level—individual, team, organization, customer, community, and shareholder. They demonstrate higher levels of trust, openness to new ideas and are more likely to share learning from past experiences with others.

Everything we've talked about thus far is necessary to create these desirable conditions. Certainly, there are other non-trivial elements of teams and culture that are not represented here. These will be addressed in Volume II. However, when integrity, as described in this book, plus a growth mindset is present, teams and organizations will embrace ever-evolving cultures that foster connection, collaboration, creativity, reflection, intellectual curiosity, ideation, innovation, and solutioning for even bigger problems—those that consume our world. Organizations of this caliber demand leaders to live in and lead from integrity. It's the only way it works.

Exploring the *Space Between*: Magic in the Middle

We realize now that discovering the Matrix isn't enough. It isn't enough to know where the entry point is. For the magic to arise we must bravely and courageously enter fully, completely, and with an insatiable appetite for blending with integrity. Within the Matrix, within the "space between" is where it begins.

The impact of making these daring choices, opens us to discovering yet a new Matrix...one that unlocks the most important and yet fundamental and crucial skill of our existence, our creativity.

As is our practice, invite yourself into a moment of Executive Reflection:

- This is your permission slip to daydream. Take 20 minutes of uninterrupted time to look out the window, take a walk-in nature, lay in the grass and look up at the sky, sit on your back porch in your favorite rocking chair or wherever you wish to be and do. Begin by pausing your inclination to do something else. In its place, invite experiencing to step forward and simply notice what appears in your imagination. Notice the experience of having this experience. This is a practice of being infinite. Express your experience in any creative form you wish: writing, drawing, pottery, painting…and so on.

- Where do I have opportunities to become more like a red rubber ball? Experiencing more of what I love. Embracing change of direction and challenges as a gift to go beyond my limited sense of knowing and seeing. And returning back to myself, feeling resourced and rejuvenated.

- Which of the seven qualities and principles do I possess? Am I a commitment for expressing these qualities openly for others to receive? How might I push beyond my comfort zone and more fully demonstrate an infinite growth mindset?

Chapter Nine
Practice with Purpose

The purpose of practice is practice.

– Chris Corrigan

Here's the thing, we are already always practicing something whether we are consciously aware or not. We may be practicing procrastination. We may be practicing avoiding the important conversation we need to have with the board, our boss, a peer, a family member or a friend. We may be practicing making excuses, placing blame while shaming others. We may be practicing feeling bad about ourselves. We may be practicing being in the same situation repeatedly as if it is Ground Hog Day. Whether we realize it or not, we are always practicing. And what, how, and who we are being while practicing shapes our performance and the experience of others that in turn shapes our brand.

Practicing this way—unconsciously and haphazardly—leaves our lives and legacies to chance. We find ourselves wondering why it seems so easy for others and not us. We simply go through our daily rituals without considering why, what, or even how our unconscious practices impact our mind, body, and energy levels. We also fail to consider the impact our attitude and mood have on our desired result. Instead, we push away other possibilities, maintain the course, and the cycle continues. We remain circling and spinning outside of the Matrix.

As we've discovered on our journey through the Matrix, we do fall into habits, routines, biases, expectations that we are unaware we have fallen into. We are blind to our own background of obviousness. What we feel is the familiarity and safety of the maintaining our equilibrium, aka, the "Comfort Zone." And with every minute, hour, and day that passes, the more deeply committed we become to maintaining this practice.

Why, you may be wondering?

Neuroscience teaches us that our minds love shortcuts; preferring routines that do not require any real time for consideration. Simply said, because it is just easy.

And as Brené Brown reminds us: When we choose comfort over courage, what is fast, fun, or easy over what is right, and when we profess but do not live our values we are not living in integrity.

If this feels impossible, it really isn't.

If you are noticing the urge to head back in the direction you came. Resist it. Stand tall facing forward in what may seem like a tornadic wind.

Yes, it takes courage, conviction, and a deep loving care for oneself to lean firmly into the trustworthy commitment we are claiming.

We must not fool ourselves by believing that failure is not an option because it is if we aren't paying attention to our intentions. When we will slip backward, which inevitably will happen, we do not have to wait till Monday morning to start again. We can begin again in this very moment. We are always at choice in our practice of integrity.

As human beings, we have the capacity—if the desire, passion, and will are present, along with an open mind and heart—to change the way our brains automatically respond. With each reoccurring practice we reconfigure and create different connection points where new habits are formed and new skills are polished.

The question then to consider is whether what you are practicing, how you are practicing, and who you are being as you practice will it get you where you want to go?

Preparing to Practice

Preparing ourselves to practice with purpose is essential. Having the will to succeed is not enough. Success is determined by how purposefully and intentionally we prepare.

Preparation begins with creating a clearing—a space and time for practice. This is followed by creating a clearing within us so that we don't fall into the drift of practicing old habits that no longer serve.

Ideally, find a spot, that in the words of famed architect, Christopher Alexander, one that "gives life and beauty." This could be inside or outside. Our surroundings and environment we practice in plays a significant role in whether we are successful or not. Our environments influence us, so taking time to find the right space. For example, if you are inside, look for a room that has natural light and preferably with windows on two walls. This allows the outside in creating a space that feels expansive.

Clear, clean, and carefully remove distractions. Adding some plants or flowers will also enliven the space. If you find yourself outside, take in nature's beauty that surrounds you.

Once we have our practice space, we can then shift our attention to preparing our minds. Our interior space of the mind requires the same attention and preparation as our external surroundings.

Barrel of Monkeys

A mind that is full is a mind that is filled with anything other than purpose.

A full mind is like a barrel of chattering, screeching monkey's all fighting for our attention. Each one jumping on top of the other to be heard, feed, and taken care of right now.

Our monkeys are relentless.

Our "monkey mind," as referenced by Buddha more than 2000 years ago, becomes an addiction that interferes with our ability to lead ourselves and others well. In fact, the more time we spend in trying to do faster, aka rapid-fire multi-tasking, the less successful we are. We are unable to be present to anything we are doing. Believing otherwise is only a trick of the mind. It is an illusion that if we are not intentional in our practice, continues to leave us on the proverbial hamster wheel.

Unfortunately, this is the gift of our society. Our society encourages us to have a "mind full." We've come to believe and value our ability to do multiple things at once. In an odd way we may even feel more worthy and important because of having mastered it. And to top it off, we are encouraged and expected to do it well even at the cost of feeling depleted, fatigued, frustrated, and longing for connection.

We've held firm to an artificial truth based on superficial evidence that points us to believe that the better we are at multi-tasking the more upward mobile we are within our organization. Because of this ungrounded assessment, we vigorously pursue it as well as we push it through our organizations, all the while we encourage others around us to learn to become more mindful.

Here's the rub: We cannot be mindful and have a mind that is full. It is simply impossible.

Taking a Break

Giving our minds, bodies, and emotions a break from the "hurry up, fast-paced, technology advanced, got-to-get-it-done, drive-thru world, where time is a luxury, and life is compounded by a constant stream of 'late-breaking-news' from around the world" is the practice of mindfulness.

Taking a break from the distractions that are imposed upon us and we accept as our reality.

Taking a break from the distractions we impose upon ourselves.

Taking a break from listening to our own internal chatter while tuning in to what is going on within us and around us. This "tuning in" and becoming self-aware of what is going on within ourselves in this moment is the practice of mindfulness.

Mindfulness is becoming aware of the chattering and screeching monkeys that are running over top one another, vying for our attention, and then choosing one to focus on, take care of, while the others are in the background. This is what is meant by quieting the mind and remaining focused. We intentionally attend to what we claim to be most important, and we stop listening to what the monkeys have to say.

When we are mindful not mind full, we are also able to discover what we need based on our personal expectations for how this world and those in it "should" operate which has been the journey laid out in this book. This very discovery, as we've learned, helps us to clearly identify how we need to take care of ourselves first, so we have the energy to take care of others.

Self-care replenishes and helps us flourish. And when we are flourishing, we have a greater chance of persevering when setbacks and challenges arise. We can more easily endure, and possibly even embrace, the setbacks, seeing them as opportunities for expanded learning.

"Tuning in" to what is happening in this moment has never been more important than it is today.

Our well-being is at risk. On the heels of the pandemic, we find ourselves less connected, driving to get more done in a shorter period of time. We are layering—not balancing—our home with our work as we continue to live in a hybrid or remote work environment. The reality is there is no place to escape when we continuously bring our work into our personal space, which we are all doing to varying degrees. Our ability to separate and compartmentalize work and home is nearly impossible. And we are experiencing the toll it takes individually and collectively across the globe.

The benefits of being mindful are plentiful:

- Eases the physical tensions in our body that makes us stiff, tight, and constrained.
- Increases our emotional range so we can respond to events, situations, and people around us instead of reacting.
- Decreases the noise in our head.
- Elevates our awareness to what is occurring in this moment with little worry or concern about what is coming next or what has just occurred.
- Aligns our intentions with our actions while being fully present to the impact our action have on others.
- Increases both our positivity and productivity.

So, if practicing mindfully can do all this, then why don't we do it?

- We hold the false belief that multi-tasking equates to efficiency and effectiveness.
- We mean to, but simply forget.
- We haven't learned how.
- We've told ourselves the story, "it isn't for me…it's a yoga thing."
- We are living a myth that mindfulness is about stopping the chatter. It isn't about stopping anything. It is about noticing that the chatter exists and the impact it has on ability to lead in integrity.

Highly successful people—including many we admire from afar, like professional athletes—are reporting that their success largely comes from mindful preparation. Slowing down the action allows us to anticipate more quickly what might arrive next with a better response time.

The same is true of professional leaders like you. Those best in their craft and discipline are the best of the best because whether they are consciously aware of it or not are indeed practicing some form of mindfulness in preparation for the big game, aka, next meeting, next one-on-one, next client engagement, and next board meeting.

Preparing to practice is a never-ending practice of creating readiness for living "a life less ordinary."

The Power of Practice

I won't lie, it isn't easy. The bonus, however, is tremendous if you step into the Matrix and step up to owning your power to choose the practices you practice moment by moment.

I invite you to become consciously aware when choosing your practices—even the small ones, such as how you enter your office. As you do notice the energy in your body and the pace of your walk. Notice where your attention falls and what distractions are allowed to immediately sneak in. Notice if you can find ease in pausing, where choice is the response instead of merely blindly reacting. From here, what you might you begin to stop, start, or continue practicing that enhances the success within yourself, your team, and your organization?

The choice is yours. Will you continue practicing the practices you've always practiced and pray for a new result? Or will you recognize and own your power to practice with purpose new practices and routines that create better futures for you and everyone you come into contact with?

As many of my clients come to realize, igniting their success begins with designing the right practices and then consciously practicing them over and over until they become the shortcuts our brain craves.

Let Your Practice Begin

This book is not a one-time read. It is meant to be read, explored, and re-read again and again. It will be a different experience every time you read or listen to it. And with each read you will be one step closer to being your most authentic, high integrity self.

The Red Thread

In this book, we successfully picked up the Red Thread; an underlying invisible connection that can be stretched or tangled but never broken. We explored, experimented and reflected on how to live in and lead with integrity daily. We took away what wasn't needed and replaced it with the fine jewels and treasures that illuminate our passion and purpose as well as that of others. We no longer see ourselves as a block of unrefined marble. We now see ourselves as Michelangelo saw David.

I saw the angel in the marble and carved it until I set it free.

Living in and leading with integrity means laying it on the line daily. It means being fully exposed, transparent, and naked. It is there in everything we do; personally, socially, and professionally. This Red Thread is a belief system that connects us to others. It's how we generate our best work and our best performance.

We carry this Red Thread through into **Discover the Matrix, Amplify Your Team and Organization's Collective Intelligence, Volume II** and throughout the **Field Book**.

I look forward to seeing you there.

Sneak Peek: Discover the Matrix, Amplify Your Team and Organization's Collective Intelligence, Volume II

Don't travel alone…meet up with others who are traveling also on the path of change, you can learn from each other a lot and together carry more learning experiences (social learning and collective intelligence.

– Nadia Grabriela Dresscher

Discover the Matrix: Amplify Your Teams and Organizations Collective Intelligence, Volume II, takes a vertical look into the "space between" teams and an organization's culture.

Within the boundaries of **Discover the Matrix, Volume II,** we bring our integrity forward as we draw our attention to the impact and the difference the quality of our leadership integrity has on those we lead, albeit to varying degrees. Here we explore the different types of intelligence within our teams and organizations. We look at the perquisites and requirements necessary to raise the quality of the culture; making the shifts in how we coordinate is necessary for our collective integrity to be experienced, intangibles to discover, and the intelligence to rise above.

Teams and organizations who successfully raise their collective intelligence resemble a beautiful masterpiece. The magic that it bestows as we stand in awe noticing the overall composition followed by the precision of each stroke. We are captivated by its significance and importance—knowing that what is being experienced in that moment is rare.

If you have been on a high-performance team, it may be easy to relive the experience. I find that it is a very sticky memory that comes easily and with incredibly fond feelings. Leaders that I have interviewed about their experience, say things like, "Ah yes, the good ole' days when a team was a team, not a group of individuals doing our own thing. We stuck together thick and thin. We had each other's back no matter the situation or challenge. We just knew what was needed and we did it." The feeling is exhilarating, the results are beyond impressive, and the ease that the individuals within the team move is indescribable. It can seem like a once in lifetime experience that magically appears with no explanation.

Like some of you, I too have had the good fortune to have been on a high-performance team who achieved repeated peak performance. Since that experience in the early 1990s, I have also led high performance-teams in both the nonprofit sector as well as within a 30,000+ employee publicly traded organization. And even more importantly, I have effectively shared these core skills with many CEOs and their executive leaders through executive and team coaching experiences; enhancing their development of themselves and their teams as they become a commitment to being high-performance.

When an executive team becomes high-performance, the organization's culture dramatically changes with it. These shifts are often subtle and occur in concurrence with the team as it moves through the team development curve; often going unnoticed by the team itself as they change how they work and how the organization coordinates.

One of my most treasured books, *The Wisdom of Teams* (Katzenbach and Smith, 1993), defines a team as "a small number of people with complementary skills who are committed to a common purpose, performance goals, and approach for which they hold themselves mutually accountable."

So, what makes a high-performance team high-performance?

My response is the same for teams as it is for high-performance leaders:

High-performance leaders, teams and organizations are very intentional in attending to the "space between."

High-performance CEOs and executive teams are constantly looking at what occurs just before it occurs and at the precise time a new image, new data, new experiences emerge. This is not dissimilar to what I learned as a child while playing with the kaleidoscope; the slower I turned the cylinder the more I could see—the more information I gathered about how the shapes and colors came together to reveal the next image. The real revelation came when I could be still enough and patient enough in that precise moment the "space between" the shapes met. It's here where the magic lies.

In **Discover the Matrix, Volume II,** we will examine how you can develop a refined awareness for sensing and mastering the skill to see and be with (and in) the "space between." This enables you to further develop the confidence and agency to act effectively within the space as you lead teams and organizations that become known are high-performance.

And when this happens, we have more engaged employees and more satisfied clients. Our culture now equals our brand.

The red thread of integrity is pulled taunt from leader through team through organizational culture through brand to the client experience. It loops over and under like an infinity sign. One feeding the other in perfect harmony where infinite possibilities exist.

And this is the repeated pattern for Igniting Success.

Sneak Peek: Discover the Matrix, Field Book

I need help...visible and invisible help...although we associate invisible help with unseen parallels—I always felt that invisible help can actually be interpreted in a very practical way. Invisible help is the help that you do not yet know you need. Sometimes that help appears, and you walk right past it and other times you actually recognize it. And this invisible help is one day made suddenly visible outside my caravan.

– David Whyte, Meditative Story Podcast,
April 22, 2021

The **Discover the Matrix Field Book** is dedicated to practicing in the "space between" where our aim is to **Bring the Intangibles to the Foreground, Making the Invisible Visible** for further vertical examination, exploration, and experimentation.

Our quest to live in and lead from Integrity requires patience, courage, a playful spirit, and a stick-to-it-ness when we are tempted to look away. Because we will be tempted to look away. And we may very well look away. How fast we notice and return to the practice is key. By returning, we persevere. Through our perseverance, we learn that your potential is infinite.

In this transcendent space we afford ourselves the luxury of being an explorer exploring old familiar territories with new eyes and from different vantage points. Our commitment to our Integrity is firm. Standing here you see more broadly, more completely, taking in the multi-levels experience that is our Self; creating a shift from the "me" to the "I."

From here, our sense of expansion invites us to see beyond what we previously had accounted for, connecting our inner and outer Integrity: The True Mark of Leadership. It amplifies the Collective Intelligence of our Teams and Organizations, and by doing so creates a culture of Integrity that is experienced by employees and customers alike.

The echoing is both heard and felt by everyone: We are a commitment to living in and leading from your truest self and our Integrity. Living and leading this way changes the conversation and more importantly changes the game.

I understand it is tempting to drift back into previously held limiting beliefs of, "Hey, I've arrived. I've completed the work in Volume 1 and Volume 2. No more practice is needed."

This is exactly why, in all honesty, I've deliberately created this **Field Book**. To force the pause, bringing attention to our habitual habit of looking past the *"space between."* The reasons are endless to why this happens, and we know it does. We are humans who yearn for deeper connection without the work which turns out to be a finite game to play. Diving fully into Field Book continues the work from **Discover the Matrix: The True Mark of Leadership, Volume I** and **Discover the Matrix: Amplify**

Your Teams and Organizations Collective Intelligence, Volume II.

So...

The **Discover the Matrix Field Book** is your illustrated manual for amplifying your leadership, your team and organizational performance. Together with the Discover the Matrix Volume I and Volume II a Leader, Team and Organization has the power to effectively change the trajectory: increased satisfaction, amplified performance, and creating a high integrity culture that matches the brand experience claimed.

More on the horizon from ANGELA CUSACK…

Once finding her expertise formulating the 'space between' Angela Cusack has found herself going deeper into working with today's highly recognized leaders, teams, and organizations.

Her work and research into what make leaders, teams and organizations standout above the rest, continues to lead her back to the fundamentals of being in and living out of our integrity. How it impacts the culture and relates to the organization's brand is what Angela plans to share in her next book, Part II of The Matrix, due to be released in 2024.

And as she does so, Angela' self-exploration isn't over. As her new discoveries become visible, she plans to share them as a way of illuminating and innovating on what is possible beyond what we might imagine. The hope is that she will inspire others to ignite their spark leading them to design a creative life worth living.

Angela lives with her husband Sean and their Havanese pup Murphy Rose Q in Lake Mary, Florida.

For the latest information visit:
www.angelacusack.co
www.ignitingsuccess.com